Study Guide

to accompany

Carson • Lapsansky-Werner • Nash

AFRICAN AMERICAN LIVES

The Struggle for Freedom

Volume I

Olivia Green
Miles College

New York Boston San Francisco
London Toronto Sydney Tokyo Singapore Madrid
Mexico City Munich Paris Cape Town Hong Kong Montreal

Study Guide to accompany *African American Lives: The Struggle for Freedom, Volume I*

ISBN: 0-321-33780-8

1 2 3 4 5 6 7 8 9 10– OPM –08 07 06 05

TABLE OF CONTENTS

CHAPTER 1 *Ancient Africa*

CHAPTER SUMMARY

Opening Vignette: African Storytelling and African American History

Africa's rich oral cultures long preserved its history and wisdom. For Africans wrenched into slavery in America, storytelling nurtured the collective memory and sustained the spirit. As a few, then many, began to write and publish their experiences, a people whose past had been officially suppressed began to regain its voice. Twentieth-century black historians insisted the African American story be included in American history. In the twenty-first century, that has come to be.

From Human Beginnings to the Rise of Egypt

Archaeologists have found the earliest human remains in eastern Africa, and today most scientists believe that human life began in that region about 160,000 years ago. Some 100,000 years later, humans began to migrate out of Africa to the Middle East and in to Asia and Australia. By 6,000 BCE, settlements along the Nile, the world's longest river, made Egypt the most densely populated part of the world.

Here, as early hydraulic engineers learned to use the predictable flooding of the Nile to irrigate crops, Egyptian civilization flourished. Ruled by pharaohs, who claimed godlike powers, the Egyptian kingdom administered labor, collected taxes, erected tombs and temples, and developed a system of writing in hieroglyphs. In the New Kingdom period (1570–1085 BCE), wars of expansion brought the peoples of Palestine and Syria in the Middle East, and Kush on the upper Nile, under Egyptian influence. For some 3,000 years Egyptian civilization dominated the lands bordering the Mediterranean Sea.

During these years, Egypt was a crossroads for trade and cultural exchange. Its importance in the ancient world was recognized by later Europeans, but only after they had mentally plucked Egypt out of Africa and Africans out of Egypt. Today scholars still argue over whether the ancient Egyptians were "black," "white," or racially mixed, and they continue to debate Egypt's influence on ancient Greece and Rome. Martin Bernal's *Black Athena* (1987) set off a furious controversy in proposing that white scholars had long suppressed the fundamental role of Egypt and Africa in western civilization. The book also strengthened African American efforts to reconnect with African origins and stimulated scholars generally to examine the concept of race. Egypt's dominance was challenged temporarily by Kush, which ruled the kingdom from 750 to 670 BCE. But in 332 BCE, its conquest by Alexander the Great signaled the end of the longest-lasting civilization in human history. Yet Egypt continued to serve as a crossroads for trade and culture. After the Romans came to dominate the Mediterranean, trade and periodic warfare accelerated the intermingling of peoples and introduced a new faith, Christianity, that spread west across North Africa and south into Nubia and Ethiopia, where it still flourishes today.

The Spread of Islam

Beginning in the seventh century, another new faith, Islam, reached Africa. It came from Arabia, where in 610 a 40-year-old merchant named Muhammad saw a vision of the angel Gabriel and began preaching. His message had great appeal: all believers are equal; through private and communal prayer, kindness and generosity, and fasting during Ramadan, anyone can embrace the One True God. Islam did not require an exclusive priesthood. It did require compassion for the poor, a rejection of alcohol and gambling, a high regard for learning, strict honesty in commercial transactions, and a mandate to convert others.

Islam spread rapidly, not only west across North Africa to Spain and south along the Red Sea, but east to India and China. Its armies stimulated the exchange of goods, ideas, and technologies, as well as religious belief. In West Africa, new urban commercial centers rose along trade routes.

The Emergence of West African Kingdoms

Islam reached West Africa by the tenth century. Here iron technology, known since 450 BCE, had made possible the tools that increased agricultural productivity and, in turn, the growth of population. Some of Africa's greatest kingdoms rose in the grasslands and fertile rainforests of the Niger River Basin.

In turn, Ghana, Mali, and Songhai thrived, their small villages and large cities supported by a flourishing trade in gold. Muslim Arabs who crossed the Sahara to Ghana brought ceramics, glass, oil lamps, and salt; the gold they sought in exchange circulated as coin throughout the Christian Mediterranean. With the trade in goods came trade in ideas and the introduction of Arabic script and numbers and the Islamic faith. In 1235 Islamic Mali rose to crush its Ghanaian overlords, and in 1307 its legendary king Mansa Musa began a reign famous for its wealth. His inland city of Timbuktu was a gateway to the Sahara and a center of Islamic scholarship and art.

In 1435 Mali lost power to the breakaway state of Songhai. A century later Songhai itself began to collapse, just as adventuresome Portuguese sailors were establishing commercial links along the African coast. While European kingdoms were centralizing, African kingdoms devolved into smaller states.

South of Songhai, Yoruba-speaking peoples established the forest kingdoms of Ife and Benin. Productive agriculture and knowledge of ironworking made them prosperous and eager to trade. The Portuguese who arrived in 1485 found a highly organized society with an absolute monarch and a people positioned to capture slaves from the interior.

Central African Kingdoms

West Africa would become one of the biggest sources of slaves shipped across the Atlantic, but Central Africa exported slaves as well. Kongo, which Europeans first encountered in 1482, was home to two million Bakong people who had migrated into central Africa. Among them were the Nok, originally from the Niger-Benue area, whose early knowledge of ironmaking made Kongo "the land of the blacksmith kings" and a lively trade center. To the south, Ndongo also thrived.

Both kingdoms, highly centralized, were also positioned to make trade agreements with the Portuguese, which would lead to a trade in slaves.

African Culture

Studying the cultures of West and Central Africa helps us to understand how enslaved Africans in the Americas refashioned themselves and built defenses against the cruelties inflicted on them. In ancient and medieval Africa, the family served as the basic unit of society, and in most villages, everyone was part of a single lineage. Each person felt linked to others, defined by relations. "Alone, a person was nobody," a historian has explained. Unlike Europeans, Africans emphasized interdependence rather than individualism. Also unlike Europe, kinship systems in Africa were largely matrilineal, a tradition that carried over into slavery, as African women continued to have influence in their families in ways not typical of European families. Many Africans practiced polygamy, and most married women were co-wives. They cultivated the land, tended livestock, and marketed surplus produce.

African religions generally recognized a supreme being or creator, as well as a pantheon of lesser gods associated with nature. Elaborate rituals showed respect for spirits in nature and for ancestors, as both were believed capable of intervening in human affairs. West Africans also believed in spirit possession—gods speaking to men and women through religious leaders and natural forces and objects. By the late fifteenth century, Islam had begun to displace traditional religions, and enslaved Africans brought a complex religious heritage to the Americas. In slavery, their spiritual traditions sustained them, and their belief in a physical and a spiritual world, coinciding with Christian beliefs, enabled a hybrid African Christianity to develop.

African societies were much like European societies in political organization: a king supported by land-owning nobles, military leaders, and priests, overseeing a bureaucracy that handled taxes and commerce. Under them were artisans and traders, and the great mass of people who tilled the soil. African societies also had slaves, largely captured enemies who worked as domestic servants and artisans. In this, African slavery differed markedly from the slavery that developed in Europe's colonies, where slaves engaged in field labor, generally for life, had no rights or protections, and passed their condition to their children through the female line.

African art, music, dance, and aesthetic expression also helped sustain Africans in slavery. Dance and music were intrinsic to communal religious observances and festivals. They enabled Africans to celebrate life together; music was not performed by individuals for an audience, as in Europe, nor were compositions attributed to a single creator. Instead, Africans improvised, and their music unfolded with antiphony, syncopation, and a percussive style in which drums played an essential role. In art Africans created beautiful objects with real functions, not paintings of scenes or individuals to be admired, although carvings of kings' likenesses commemorated royal power. West and Central African sculptures and carvings testify to the skills of African artisans, and their delicately carved ivories were much sought after by early European traders.

LEARNING OBJECTIVES

Students should be able to

- describe the human origins in East Africa.
- explain the debate over the race of early Egyptians.
- discuss the characteristics and history of early African civilizations.
- discuss the role of Islam in African history.

IDENTIFICATIONS

Explain the significance of each of the following:

1. griots
2. Yoruba
3. hominids
4. Australopithecine
5. paleoanthropologists
6. "out of Africa" theory
7. pharoahs
8. *Black Athena: The Afroasiatic Roots of Classical Civilization*
9. lineage
10. Nubia
11. Kush
12. Islam
13. Muhammad
14. Ghana
15. Mali
16. Songhai
17. Sundiata
18. Mansa Musa

19. Timbuktu

20. Nok

21. Ndongo

MULTIPLE CHOICE QUESTIONS

1. Because most African societies did not have a written language, there were storytellers, called oral historians, who passed information down through the ages. These oral historians were known as
    A. pharaohs.
    B. sultans.
    C. griots.
    D. caliphs.

2. This practice of oral storytelling by Africans was brought to America by enslaved people. It was continued through many generations here in America because
    A. slaves had little opportunities to publish written accounts as it was against the master's law to teach slaves to read and write.
    B. slaves wanted to keep the ancient traditions alive.
    C. they wanted their descendants to learn about their heritage and traditions.
    D. All of the above statements are true.

3. Charles Darwin proposed in his book, *Descent of Man*, published in 1871, that Africa was probably the birthplace of humankind. This notion offended Europeans because
    A. they saw their own race as being superior to that of the African.
    B. some Europeans maintained that human life began in Europe - particularly in Germany's Neander Valley.
    C. Both A and B are correct.
    D. A is correct but not B.

4. Scientists who study human origins discovered that *Homo erectus*, or upright human, dated back about 1.8 million years. They further stated that *Homo sapiens*, meaning wise humans, originated in Africa about 120,000 to 160,000 years ago. These scientists are called
   A. anthropologists.
   B. archaeologists.
   C. paleoanthropologists.
   D. zoologists.

5. The debates by scholars over whether or not Egypt is in Africa, or whether Egyptians are black people is still the topic of passionate debate today. Martin Bernal states in his book, *Black Athena: The Afroasiatic Roots of Classical Civilization,* that
   A. white scholars have suppressed the role that Egyptians and Semitic peoples played in the making of Greek civilization.
   B. these ancient dark-skinned peoples invented the mathematics, philosophy, and religion on which classical Greece was built.
   C. modern Western civilization owes a great debt to ancient Africa.
   D. All of the above statements are true.

6. The debates also center around the skin color of this queen of Egypt who greatly influenced Roman leaders during the Classical period.
   A. Aphrodite
   B. Tutankhamen
   C. Cleopatra
   D. Hatshepsut

7. These dark-skinned people lived in Kush, a territory along the Nile River in what is known as Upper Egypt. They eventually took control over Egypt by 750 BCE, only to control it less than 100 years. The people were called
   A. Nubians.
   B. Israelis.
   C. Palestinians.
   D. Philistines.

8. This monotheistic religion has its beginning in Saudi Arabia in the early seventh century and made a tremendous impact on Africa and the rest of world.
   A. Christianity
   B. Judaism
   C. Hinduism
   D. Islam

9. The religion in question #8 contains all of the following tenets <u>EXCEPT</u>
   A. its founder was Muhammad.
   B. the Qu'ran is the holy book.
   C. Jerusalem is the holy city.
   D. followers fast from sunrise to sunset during the month of Ramadan.

10. Three Sudanese kingdoms became wealthy due to their location in or adjacent to the gold region of West Africa. Another reason for their wealth is due to the taxes imposed on Arab merchants as they either passed through or traded with the Sudanese kings. All of the following are Sudanese kingdoms EXCEPT
    A. Kongo.
    B. Ghana.
    C. Mali.
    D. Songhai.

11. Mandingo warriors helped this king of Mali overthrow the warlords of Ghana in 1235 at the Battle of Kirina. As a result, Ghana ceased to exist and this ruler became king of the Islamic state of Mali.
    A. Sundiata
    B. Tutankhamen
    C. Ramses II
    D. Shaka Zulu

12. This king of Mali was the first West African leader to convert to Islam. When making his pilgrimage to Mecca in 1324, he won fame when he made a 3,500-mile trek across the Sahara accompanied by an entourage of 50,000. He impressed the world by displaying Mali's wealth and dispensing lavish gifts of gold as he made his way to the holy land.
    A. Ramses
    B. Mansa Musa
    C. Akhenatops
    D. Tutankhamen

13. This city was built by the Songhai rulers and became the center for Islamic learning in Africa. It was described by Leo Africanus, a noted European writer and traveler, in his *History and Description of Africa* as being a "paradise."
    A. Alexandria
    B. Zimbabwe
    C. Timbuktu
    D. Baghdad

14. In ancient and medieval Africa, as elsewhere, this institution served as the basic unit of society.
    A. The family
    B. The clan
    C. The village
    D. The kingdom

15. As in almost every human society, this institution's thought and practice in Africa made life's challenges meaningful and bearable.
    A. Music
    B. Religion
    C. Art
    D. Dance

16. In African societies the importance of the individual is subordinate to the importance of the group or community-at-large. The concept of *individualism* did not exist in Africa.
    A. True
    B. False
    C. Partly true
    D. Partly false

17. African societies included slaves. Slavery existed at the same time in Europe, Asia, and Africa. The nature of slavery that existed in Africa was not like the *chattel* slavery that later existed in America. The following rules and protections applied EXCEPT
    A. Slaves could obtain an education, marry, and raise a family.
    B. Slavery was not a lifelong condition in Africa.
    C. Slavery did not automatically pass on to a slave woman's children.
    D. Slaves could count on decent treatment from their owners.
    E. All of the above statements are true

THOUGHT QUESTIONS

1. What comparisons do you see between the list of African Proverbs found in the First Person document on page 21 with proverbs found in the Christian Bible?

2. Why do you suppose Leo Africanus could find such marvelous wonders about Africa in his book, *History and Description of Africa* published in Italian in 1550, then translated into English and published again in 1600? However, experts, during that era, and still presently, refer to Africa as being the "dark continent" and claimed Africa to be void of any intellectual or scholarly pursuits.

ANSWER KEY MULTIPLE CHOICE QUESTIONS

1. C
2. D
3. C
4. C
5. D
6. C
7. A
8. D
9. C
10. A
11. A
12. B
13. C
14. A
15. B
16. A
17. E

CHAPTER 2 *Africa and the Atlantic World*

CHAPTER SUMMARY

Opening Vignette: King Nomimansa Meets Diego Gomes

In 1456, under the pretense of negotiating a commercial treaty, Portuguese ship captain Diego Gomes seized twenty-two of King Nomimansa's people as slaves, prefiguring a tragic aspect of European-African relations that would unfold for centuries to come.

Africa and Europe: The Fateful Connection

In the 1400s, innovations in the technology of navigation revolutionized the Atlantic world, first allowing the Portuguese to expand their trade network south along the west coast of Africa and to seize uninhabited coastal islands, where they experimented with the cultivation of sugarcane. The increased availability of sugar made it much sought after, and by 1500 the Portuguese were importing about five thousand African slaves annually, to work in a new form of agriculture they developed. This plantation system was marked by large landholding, forced labor of gangs of slaves, and a cash crop that commanded steep prices in distant places.

Africa and the Rising Atlantic World

Christopher Columbus's voyage across the Atlantic, in 1492, shifted the momentum of European expansion from the Portuguese to the Spanish. Following the dictates of mercantilism, colonies were intended to enrich home countries, and the successful experiment with sugarcane cultivation on the islands off Africa proved a model for the colonization of the New World. To supply the nearly insatiable demand for plantation labor, Europeans ultimately transported more than 10 million Africans out of their homelands—the largest forced migration in human history. Human slavery was not unknown in Africa, where black rulers had long raided and sold their enemies. The transport of slaves to the east, to Muslim societies around the Red Sea and Indian Ocean, equaled the transport west in numbers, but these captured Africans served as concubines and personal attendants, and had some rights. Slaves bound for the plantations of the New World, in contrast, were regarded by European Christians as nonhuman possessions, an inferior species better off toiling in the fields than living where they were born. In the Americas, Europeans believed, African "savages" could be "civilized" through exposure to Christianity and European culture.

At first the Spanish and Portuguese tried to enslave native peoples for plantation labor, but the natives' high death rate from European diseases to which they had no immunity, and the ease with which they could escape in regions with which they were familiar, led the colonizers to look to Africa. Soon Africans were hacking out plantations from New World forests. As the Spanish, Portuguese, and English introduced additional cash crops—coffee, tobacco, rice, and indigo—they engaged in a fierce competition for the slave trade, which was accelerating the procurement of slaves in Africa. Whereas Europeans had formerly traded with Africans, they now traded in Africans. African kings could not anticipate the consequences of the trade agreements they made and, with European guns, turned to waging war against each other to secure slaves. The maelstrom of conflict thus unleashed depopulated Africa's heartlands. Europeans, too, waged war against each other for control of the slave trade. By the 1790s, England emerged as the foremost slave-trading nation in all of Europe.

The Trauma of Enslavement

For Africans seized in this violent trade, life was miserable and short. Captured in village homelands, they were marched in coffles hundreds of miles to coastal forts, where African sellers drove hard bargains for what the Europeans called "black gold." Deliberately mixed with Africans from many regions—to prevent communication and cooperation—they were thrust onto slave ships. Now they knew they would be separated from home and family forever, and Europeans knew this was the moment when the chance of suicide or uprising was the greatest.

Then began the horrendous "middle passage"—the journey across the Atlantic to the Americas. As many as three hundred Africans were shackled together in half-decks no more than four feet apart. The stench of the living, the shrieks and groans of the dying, were an inconceivable horror. Inadequate nourishment and lack of water produced mind-numbing dehydration and fomented the spread of disease. Enslaved African women were regularly raped. Captives who protested or planned uprisings were tortured to death as examples. Perhaps no more than two of every three captured Africans survived to land on the other side of the Atlantic.

Olaudah Equiano, whose chronicle of enslavement is related as emblematic of the experience of many, remembered this part of the journey as the worst. Sold to a Virginia planter and taken to a small plantation upriver from the Chesapeake Bay, he now "had no person to speak to that I could understand." The ultimate trauma of enslavement was utter isolation. Africans sold in the New World were worked to death. On average, that took just seven years.

Africans in North America

In the 1500s, the early years of Spanish exploration, Africans occupied a respected status as members of expeditions valued for their skills in soldiering and in negotiating with native peoples. By 1580, some 45,000 of them had arrived in Spanish colonies in Florida and present-day New Mexico. Though they did much of the back-breaking work of field labor, transport, and fort and church construction, the scarcity of capable workers and skilled linguists gave enslaved Africans a higher status and a greater degree of freedom than they would have in the later English colonies. The example of the black Moor Estévan, who crossed the continent with Cabeza de Vaca in the 1530s, is an example.

In early North America, cultures converged and definitions of slavery blurred. On both the east and west coasts, Africans forged sexual unions and raised children with Native Americans and with Spanish people, and, in turn, genetic blending broke down traditional social categories. The coming domination of the English, however, would change attitudes toward Africans and the practice of slavery itself.

LEARNING OBJECTIVES

Students should be able to

- describe the first interactions between Europeans and sub-Saharan Africa.
- explain how Europeans altered the ancient institution of slavery.
- discuss the origins of the plantation system.
- describe the ordeal of the "middle passage."
- compare the ways that slavery differed among Spanish, Portuguese, and English slave plantations.

IDENTIFICATIONS

Explain the significance of each of the following:

1. middle passage

2. Prince Henry the Navigator

3. mercantilism

4. Olaudah Equiano

5. diasporo

6. coffles

7. barracoons

8. Estevan

9. creole

10. Juan Ponce de Leon

11. Guale Indians

12. Hernando de Soto

13. Mandingo

MULTIPLE CHOICE QUESTIONS

1. These people were eager to sign slave trade arrangements with the Portuguese traders. They lived near the mouth of the Gambia River during the Songhai kingdom. The African people in question were the
   A. Swahili.
   B. Bantu.
   C. Mandingo.
   D. Zuni.

2. Captured Africans were sold into slavery by tribal kings to Portuguese traders in exchange for which of the following?
   A. Damask cloth
   B. Brass pots
   C. Glass beads
   D. Swords and knives
   E. All of the above

3. Which of the following means was <u>most often</u> used by European traders to obtain slaves from Africa?
   A. The raid-and-trade tactic
   B. Barter with the tribal chieftain
   C. Marauding Europeans made war against Africans on offshore islands and seized some of them.
   D. All of the above

4. This term is used to refer to the forced removal of a group of people from their homeland.
   A. Diaspora
   B. Exodus
   C. Migration
   D. Transmigration

5. For how long a period of time did the forced removal of Africans last?
   A. Fifty years
   B. Four centuries
   C. One hundred years
   D. Five hundred years

6. The ancestors of present day African Americans came mainly from this part of Africa:
   A. Sub Saharan Africa.
   B. Northern Africa.
   C. South Africa.
   D. West and Central Africa.

7. After being captured in an interior area, slaves were chained together by the neck and marched brutally to the coastal area to wait for the arrival of the next slave ship. This arrangement of the trek is known as the
   A. African trek.
   B. pilgrimage.
   C. coffle.
   D. sentimental journey.

8. The holding station for captured Africans was called the
   A. barracoon or factory.
   B. slave pen.
   C. bush country.
   D. rainforest.

9. The voyage from Africa to the Americas carrying captured slaves was known as the
   A. Mandela March.
   B. Middle passage.
   C. Crusades.
   D. Bataan Death March.

10. According to experts, the approximate number of African slaves exported across the Atlantic between the years 1520 – 1870 is
    A. 50,345,000.
    B. 7,356,000.
    C. 75,873,000.
    D. 11,698,000.

11. The number of Africans who died before reaching the intended destination of the slave traders has been estimated as high as 920,000 to several million. Their deaths were due to
    A. fatalities during the capture.
    B. the march to the coast.
    C. long confinement on the coast.
    D. the ocean crossing.
    E. all of the above.

12. This captured Ibo-born male, at age 10, was sold into slavery, endured the Atlantic voyage, the internal auction blocks, slavery for ten years, liberation, and then marriage to an English woman. He later wrote a much-published account of his experiences and documented the miseries that the slave trade was bringing to his unfortunate countrymen. He was
    A. Diago Gomes.
    B. Olaudah Equiano.
    C. Ruy do Siqueira.
    D. Estevan.

13. The circumstances of slaves sold in Muslim lands differed markedly from those sold in the New World. Which of the reasons cited below is NOT true?

A. Muslims wanted slaves who could serve as porters, soldiers, concubines (mistresses), cooks and personal attendants rather than as field hands. Consequently more slave women were sent to Muslim countries than men.
B. Masters in the Americas viewed slaves as non-human possessions; Muslim masters saw bondsmen and women as people even though Moslems still treated them harshly.
C. In Muslim countries, slaves had more rights than in the Americas. Some slaves could voluntarily choose the Islamic religion while others were forced to do so. Muslim masters freed more of their slaves than American masters did.
D. Islam emphasized a universal community that transcended race, so former African slaves who embraced the faith found it easier to feel united spiritually with other Muslims. This was not the case in the Americas.
E. All of the above are true statements.

14. This dark skinned Moroccan-born male slave was referred to as “a black,” “a Moor,” “an Arabian,” or “an Atlantic Creole.” He traveled with three Spaniards from Spanish Florida to other locations inward and served as a valuable guide, interpreter and a negotiator with hostile Native American tribes. He was not treated as a slave but was valued for his skills during this journey. He was

A. Estevan.
B. Olaudah Equiano.
C. Diago Gomes.
D. Ruy do Siqueira.

15. What is true about Native American relationships with African slaves?

A. Native Americans saw African slaves as very different, and quickly adopted racist views similar to the British.
B. Being very proud culturally, Native Americans refused to mix sexually with slaves.
C. Native Americans often provided refuge to escaping slaves and some areas saw extensive race mixing.
D. None of the above statements are true.

16. Which Europeans brought the first Africans to the Americas?

A. The Dutch
B. The Spanish
C. The British
D. The Germans

THOUGHT QUESTIONS

1. After reading the First Person document entitled *A Portuguese Courtier Describes Enslaved Africans* on page 31 of the text, do you believe you might commit suicide rather than be separated from your family and live as a slave based on the tales you had been told about American slavery?

2. Based on the First Person documents in this chapter that describe the cruelties and inhumane treatment of slaves during the Atlantic crossing, would you be in favor of paying reparations to Africans for the history of slavery as well as issuing an apology? These measures were debated at a United Nations conference in Africa in the year 2001.

ANSWER KEY MULTIPLE CHOICE QUESTIONS

1. C.
2. E
3. B
4. A
5. B
6. D
7. C
8. A
9. B
10. D
11. E
12. B
13. E
14. A
15. C
16. B

CHAPTER 3 *Africans in Early North America, 1619-1726*

CHAPTER SUMMARY

Opening Vignette: Anthony Johnson and His Family in the Early Chesapeake

The experience of Anthony Johnson and his family exemplifies changes in Chesapeake life and labor during the first century of white settlement. An African delivered to the Virginia colony by a Portuguese slave ship in 1621, he labored on a tobacco plantation for twenty years, married, and gained his freedom and a farm. Ironically, by the time he died in 1670, his children and their families had fewer opportunities, their lives increasingly restrained by race-based laws and precedents defining slavery and restricting free blacks.

The First Africans in English North America

Africans were present at the beginning of almost every European settlement in the Americas. While the vast majority were sold as slaves in the colonies of Spain and Portugal, a few came to English plantation owners along the Chesapeake Bay, where their labor was needed in the tobacco fields. Through the first century after the founding of Virginia in 1607, however, most field laborers were white indentured servants who contracted their labor for a set number of years. While a few Africans were slaves in Puritan Massachusetts and in Rhode Island, New Englanders' connections to slavery were mainly through trade. They sent grain, wood, and fish to the large slave plantations of the West Indies, consumed slave-produced sugar, coffee, rice, tobacco, and indigo, and built and sailed the ships that carried all these goods—and, after the late 1690s, slaves.

In New Netherlands, founded by the Dutch in 1624, slavery took root more firmly and deeply than it did in the seventeenth-century Chesapeake. As the Dutch controlled the slave trade, New Netherlands (later New York) became the largest slave importation center in North America. Africans labored on Dutch farms along the Hudson River, but they had opportunities to gain their freedom, buy land, and mix with white neighbors. Swedes and Finns brought Africans to Delaware, and after 1664, when the English defeated the Dutch and took control of the mid-Atlantic colonies, slaveholding increased. Even in Pennsylvania, where slave ownership conflicted with Quaker beliefs, Africans were bought and sold as laborers, and Philadelphia became a slave trading and slaveholding hub. Though Pennsylvania, like all the colonies, was enmeshed in the Atlantic basin human trade network, most Quakers held only a few slaves and tried to treat them humanely. In contrast, the colony of South Carolina began with a ready-made plantation system, transferred wholesale from Barbados by English slave owners.

The Fateful Transition

By the end of the seventeenth century, in England's Chesapeake and southern colonies, a pivotal changeover had occurred. In the early years, slavery had been just one of many sources of labor; now it was the foundation of the economy—the primary means of producing goods and providing services.

The English got a late start in the slave-based plantation system, but after the 1640s English settlers in Barbados and other Caribbean islands replicated the sugar and coffee plantations of the Spanish and Portuguese, with their gangs of African laborers. Defeating the Dutch in 1664, the English began to dominate the New World slave trade, and English and New England ship captains brought slaves directly from Africa to North America.

In South Carolina, by the 1720s, most field laborers were enslaved Africans, and two-thirds of imported Africans were male, most in their teens and early twenties. Planters bought large volumes of slaves and worked them mercilessly, treating them as replaceable commodities. As the number of slaves rose, the slave system grew harsher, and the colonial legislature permitted punishments unheard of in other colonies.

In the Chesapeake, Bacon's Rebellion in 1676, which united landless whites, free blacks, and runaway slaves in an uprising against the planter aristocracy, drove plantation owners to seek a permanent labor force with no claims to liberty or equality. At the same time, conditions in England improved, and fewer English men and women were willing to be indentured servants. As the slave trade flourished and the supply of Africans increased, Chesapeake colonists relied more heavily than before on black slave labor.

But societies with large numbers of slaves were dangerous. Slave revolts erupted in Jamaica and Bardados in the seventeenth century, and in 1712 in New York. Even severe punishments could not put an end to violence or fear.

Defining Slavery, Defining Race

Even before the end of the seventeenth century, another profound shift had taken place as a series of legal decisions in the Chesapeake created racial slavery and slave codes. Race-based punishments and privileges first appeared in 1630; by the 1640s, country courts were recording sales of Africans and their children into lifelong bondage. In 1662, the ambiguous legal status of Africans ended with a Virginia law stating that children "borne in this country" should be slave or free, depending on the condition of the mother. Here were the two crucial distinctions that set enslavement of Africans throughout the Americas apart from slavery elsewhere in the world: slave status was lifelong, and it was inherited through slave mothers. By reversing English legal doctrine stating that a child's status was determined by paternity, this 1662 law also guaranteed that the black labor force would reproduce itself and made African women even more vulnerable to white men's sexual exploitation. Religious and cultural prejudices had a role in this legal definition of slavery, as did the economic advantages of consigning blacks to lifelong labor in the booming tobacco fields.

New statutes also restricted the rights of free blacks, preventing them from acquiring land and banning interracial marriage. Conversion to Christianity as an avenue to freedom was cut off, and slave owners were prohibited from freeing slaves unless they also transported them out of the colony. South Carolina's slave code, consolidated in 1712, was the most severe in English North America, but interracial sex between white men and black women was tolerated. As on the Caribbean islands, the mulatto population grew.

Slavery and Race North of the Chesapeake

In contrast to the Chesapeake and Carolinas, slave labor in the northern colonies was not the basis of the economy, and New England never specifically legislated perpetual and hereditary slavery. African bondspeople had some rights: they could sue and testify in court, make contracts, bear arms, and acquire property. After the English conquered New Netherlands, however, they began passing laws that were institutionalized as a slave code in 1702. Even in Quaker Pennsylvania a slave code slowly took shape.

Beyond English Boundaries

Slavery in the North American colonies of Spain and France differed from English colonial slavery. Africans had lived in Spanish Florida from the first, mixing with Spaniards and Indians. Castilian law offered avenues out of slavery, and the Catholic church welcomed African converts. In *Slave and Citizen* (1946), historian Frank Tannenbaum noted the paradox of African slaves receiving better treatment in the autocratic colonies of Spain than in English colonies with representative government. He pointed to Catholic attitudes and Roman law as explanation. But elsewhere in Spain's empire, wherever slaves outnumbered the white settlers, they were treated harshly.

Florida was something of a slave sanctuary, however. As an outpost in Spain's empire, it was neglected, and local administrators tolerated a racially mixed population that attracted South Carolina's slaves and drew the enmity of its white elites. As slaves escaped to freedom in Florida, a border warfare between the two colonies went on for years, erupting into battles during Queen Anne's War (1702) and the Yamasee War of 1715, in which runaway slaves joined the Indian uprising.

The French colonies of Canada had little use for African slaves, but after France claimed the vast North American interior, the French used slave labor to build settlements along the Gulf coast. In 1718 they established Louisiana as a tobacco- and indigo-producing colony, building its port city of New Orleans almost entirely with coerced labor, mostly African. Slavery was the basis for the economy in Louisiana, but as in Spanish Florida, African men mingled extensively with Indian women, and soldiers formed liaisons with African women. Though France's legal code forbade interracial marriage, it was hardly enforced on the lower Mississippi frontier.

LEARNING OBJECTIVES

Students should be able to

- outline the gradual emergence of the institution of slavery.
- discuss the transition in England's southern colonies from a society in which slavery was one source of labor to a society in which slavery was the foundation of the economy.
- identify how the law was used to solidify slavery.
- describe the differences in slavery among British, Dutch, Spanish, and French colonies in North America.
- identify the ways in which Africans resisted slavery in North America.

IDENTIFICATIONS

Explain the significance of each of the following:

1. Jamestown
2. 1619
3. indentured servitude
4. Plymouth Colony
5. Anthony Johnson
6. Mary Johnson
7. Francis Payne
8. Jan Rodriguez
9. Society of Friends
10. miscegenation
11. England's Charles II
12. Barbadians
13. Nathaniel Bacon
14. Bacon's Rebellion
15. Pequot Indians
16. *partus sequitur ventrem*
17. Black Alice
18. Tuscaroras
19. Robert de LaSalle
20. French Louisiana

MULTIPLE CHOICE QUESTIONS

1. Where was the first permanent British settlement in North America?
    - A. New Orleans
    - B. Plymouth Colony
    - C. Jamestown
    - D. St. Augustine

2. In what year were Africans first brought to the British settlement of Virginia?
    - A. 1607
    - B. 1665
    - C. 1620
    - D. 1619

3. The first Africans brought to British Virginia were treated as
    - A. indentured servants.
    - B. concubines.
    - C. slaves.
    - D. yeoman farmers.

4. The second British settlement in North America was established in this year.
    - A. 1607
    - B. 1665
    - C. 1620
    - D. 1619

5. This African American, from the Kongo-Angola region, was brought to America and served as a slave on a tobacco plantation in Virginia for 20 years before gaining his freedom. While still a slave, he married a woman who resided and worked on the same plantation, with whom he shared 40 years together. Once liberated, they bought a home and eventually owned 250 acres of tobacco land, and passed it on to their children who owned twice as much land. His name was
    - A. Francis Payne.
    - B. Anthony Johnson.
    - C. Nathaniel Bacon.
    - D. Jan Rodriguez.

6. This term refers to interracial sexual contact.
    - A. Mulatto
    - B. Miscegenation
    - C. Integration
    - D. Creole

7. During the early years of the African settlement in North America, it was not so rare to find marriages between African males and white women and also between Africans and Native Americans. How would the British have categorized a person of dual white and black parentage?
   A. The child was always considered the same race as the mother.
   B. Anyone with black blood was automatically considered black.
   C. That person would be adopted into white society if his or her skin color was light enough.
   D. All of the above.

8. What is true about Native American relationships with African slaves?
   A. Native Americans saw African slaves as very different, and quickly adopted racist views similar to the British.
   B. Being very proud culturally, Native Americans refused to mix sexually with slaves.
   C. Native Americans often provided refuge to escaping slaves and some areas saw extensive race mixing.
   D. None of the above statements are true.

9. Who brought the first Africans to North America?
   A. The Dutch
   B. The Spanish
   C. The British
   D. The French

10. Slavery in the New England area differed greatly from slavery in the Chesapeake area during the early seventeenth century. In the New England area, slaves could do which of the following that they could not do in the Chesapeake?
    A. Slaves had opportunities to gain their freedom.
    B. Slaves could buy land.
    C. Slaves could mix with white neighbors.
    D. All of the above.

11. What is NOT generally a characteristic of chattel slavery, which began to develop in the British colonies in the 1660s?
    A. Slaves lost many of their legal rights, but they could still be married.
    B. The condition of the mother dictates the condition of the child.
    C. Slaves could not own property, vote, or bear arms.
    D. Being a Christian had no effect on a slave's status.

12 In this rebellion, which took place in 1676 in Virginia, runaway slaves, free blacks, indentured servants, and poor whites united and rebelled against the planter aristocracy because they supported the Governor's stance, which would keep the little man from moving further into the interior area. Ironically this rebellion caused slavery to become more entrenched in the Chesapeake area. The rebellion was called

A. Shays Rebellion.
B. Stono Rebellion.
C. New York Rebellion.
D. Bacon's Rebellion.

13. What statement is true about miscegenation in European colonies?

A. Because of the extreme racism of the British, racial mixing never occurred.
B. Miscegenation was more extensive and accepted in French and Spanish colonies.
C. Less racial mixing between blacks and Native Americans occurred in Spanish colonies.
D. None of the above statements are true.

14. How did the lives of black women differ from black men's under slavery? Black women were

A. limited to domestic labor only, as whites did not think that women should do field work.
B. only allowed to work in the fields, although at very different tasks than men.
C. separated from men at an early age, so that white masters could control the "breeding" process.
D. under constant threat of sexual exploitation.

15. What African characteristics did second generation slaves lose in America?

A. Language and ethnic identity.
B. Elements of family structure and concepts of self worth.
C. They generally adopted European practices and shunned all African ways.
D. None of the above statements are true.

16. How were enslaved Africans employed in the Spanish colony of St. Augustine?

A. Soldiers
B. Agricultural workers
C. House servants
D. All of the above

17. How were slaves in the Spanish colony of St. Augustine different than slaves under British rule?

A. St. Augustine slaves were treated far worse that slaves under British rule?
B. They had some social standing and power from their positions and church membership.
C. The Spanish considered slavery to be a temporary condition and freed all slaves after five years of service.
D. Spanish slaves were considered the social and political equals to whites in the colony.

THOUGHT QUESTIONS

1. Based on the First Person documents presented in this chapter as well as the narrative in the text, what are your thoughts on the origins of race-based slavery?

2. Lawmakers used slave codes to outlaw interracial marriages. Why do you think the lawmakers were so much against interracial marriages between the years 1619 to 1726? Why are many people against interracial marriages today?

ANSWER KEY MULTIPLE CHOICE QUESTIONS

1. C
2. D
3. A
4. C
5. B
6. B
7. B
8. C
9. B
10. D
11. A
12. D
13. B
14. D
15. A
16. D
17. B

CHAPTER 4 *Africans in Bondage: Early Eighteenth Century To The American Revolution*

CHAPTER SUMMARY

Opening Vignette: Venture Smith Defies the Colonial Slave System

Broteer, son of a Guinean king, was sold into slavery at age eight. But he never accepted enslavement. As an adult, now called Venture Smith and living in New England, he attacked masters, ran away, and worked on his own time to purchase freedom for himself and his family. His life reveals slave resistance. Though few achieved what Smith did, they inspired hope for many.

Colonial Slavery at High Tide

As planters replaced white indentured servants with African slaves, slave imports soared and field labor in the southern colonies became largely black, especially after Georgia ended its ban on slavery. In the coastal lowlands, planters relied on African knowledge for rice cultivation. African labor made owners rich, but Africans died in great numbers. Planters imported even more slaves, so that at the end of the colonial era, one-third of South Carolina slaves were Africa-born. By contrast, in the Chesapeake masters also worked slaves harder, but the proportion of America-born slaves rose. Big plantations gave slaves opportunitics for community and family life. As the gender ratio evened out, slave fertility rose, and so did the ratio of slave births over deaths; thus the slave population increased.

On plantations, some slaves acquired skills and did specialized tasks, as did slaves who worked in cities. But most slaves—men and women—labored in the fields. Women also labored in households, and were under the constant threat of sexual aggression by white men. In raping slave women, white men also asserted power over black men, inflicting emotional scars on victims and all who cared about them. Some relationships between white men and black women were consensual, and slave women could possibly use these liaisons to leverage advantages for their children. Nevertheless, these children, even if viewed affectionately by white fathers, rarely found acceptance in white society.

North of the Chesapeake, slaves comprised only five percent of the population. Some, like Venture Smith, possessed valuable skills and could hire out their free time. Their work was less harsh and more tolerable than the work of southern slaves, but they were isolated from other Africans. Some formed "abroad marriages" with slaves in other households. Unfortunately, children from these unions were often sold away from mothers. In the North, slaves more rapidly became a part of a composite American culture, contributing, for example, West African knowledge of smallpox inoculation that reduced epidemics. Yet while northern colonists had few slaves, they had strong economic links to slavery through trade and consumption.

Negotiated Bondage

Although Europeans rationalized their involvement in slavery by maintaining that Africans were subhuman heathens born for labor, masters found that they could not easily command slaves' labor. Despite law, terror, and torture, slaves had strategies for defiance. They shammed sickness, broke tools, dropped dishes, slowed down their work pace, pretended ignorance, and pilfered food and household goods. Securing their labor was always a contest of wills. Some masters treated slaves leniently; some used the whip; some used a tasking system that allowed slaves control over their own time when they finished assigned tasks. Those who could cultivate their own gardens and sell produce found some satisfaction in existence, and were less likely to run away.

Slaves allowed to form families were also less likely to run away, but advertisements in colonial newspaper testify to thousands of runaway cases. Most runaways disguised themselves, trying to pass as Indians or as free blacks. But many were caught and punished; some returned on their own. A few survived briefly in hidden sanctuaries called *maroon settlements.*

And a few slaves resisted violently, murdering masters or organizing rebellions. In 1730, 300 Virginia slaves staged an uprising and fled. In 1739, about 100 South Carolina slaves marched toward the Florida frontier, burning and plundering plantations along the way. A wave of revolts in New Jersey and New York in 1740-41 was marked by arson.

Afro-Floridians and Afro-Louisianans

Whereas the English colonies in North America established an elaborate slave system by the mid-eighteenth century, in Spanish Florida and French Louisiana slavery was less rigid, characterized by racial intermingling that allowed communities of free Africans to form. In Florida, African Francisco Menéndez, established the first free black town in North America, known as Mose, north of St. Augustine. Mose was a sanctuary for slaves escaping from South Carolina, and despite English attacks, the region was home to 3,000 black people by 1763, when Florida passed to England; one-quarter were free.

Louisiana was the only North American colony that started out with a black majority, and in this raw frontier wilderness French planters had to make concessions to enslaved Africans and nearby Indians, often playing them against each other. Here Africans could gain privileges and positions of authority. Some learned artisan skills; others, with the right to sell their own produce, established an economy of their own. But many still escaped to the Mississippi interior. After Louisiana passed to Spain in 1763, hundreds of slaves used the Spanish policy of *coartación* to gain freedom. At the end of the Spanish era, 900 free blacks lived in New Orleans, which comprised nearly 10 percent of its black population, a proportion surpassed in North America only in Florida.

Becoming African American

Broteer became Venture Smith; Olaudah Equiano became Gustavus Vasa, then Jacob: the replacement of birth names with slave names was often just the first step in the transformation of identity that came with enslavement. Two parallel processes also shaped the transition:

encounters among people from different parts of Africa and encounters between black slaves and white masters. There were regional variations, but everywhere slaves' lives depended on their ability to adapt.

At first slaves retained their African religions, but after the Great Awakening gave rise to an emotional style of worship that Africans found appealing, they adopted Christianity, taking comfort in the Christian message of equality and hope. Yet they interwove African spiritual practices into their faith, singing English hymns with an African rhythm. A few Africans who came to North America as Muslims retained their Islamic beliefs.

Aesthetic expression in music, dance, and body adornment also sustained Africans in slavery. Their singing and shout songs were testaments to their African spirit. Experiments with hairstyles and coverings were an outlet for retaining individuality. Knowledge of dyes added color to their clothing; brass and beads adorned their bodies. Stories from Africa, such as tales about the trickster spider Anansi, kept spirits alive.

By the eve of the American Revolution, Africans had begun to develop a new collective identity as African Americans. The merger of traditions can be seen in the slave celebration of Pentecost, known as Pinkster Day or Negro Election Day. At the same time, Euro-Americans were adapting to African ways—in agricultural techniques, medical knowledge, diet and food preparation, and even language and speech patterns.

Black Americans on the Eve of the American Revolution

Very few Africans achieved freedom, especially after the 1690s when colonial legislatures, even in the North, began to restrict owners' rights to free their slaves. Yet periodic wars offered opportunities, as slaves who volunteered for the militia were promised freedom. At the outbreak of the American Revolution, there were a few thousand free blacks in the South and about 4,000 in the North.

Africans did have a few white allies. Pennsylvania Quakers had first protested slavery in 1688. In the 1730s, Quaker Benjamin Lay called attention to slavery's evils, and in the 1750s another wave of Quaker reformers sought to remove slave traders and owners from the Society of Friends. John Woolman argued in *Some Considerations on the Keeping of Negroes* (1753) that Africans were equal in God's eyes. And Anthony Benezet, who taught black children, slave and free, to read, also challenged the proslavery argument that Africans were inferior. On the eve of revolution, however, few Americans saw the irony of demanding their own freedom while subjugating slaves.

LEARNING OBJECTIVES

Students should be able to

- discuss how slaves struggled to survive and resist slavery.
- explain the factors leading to the increase in the slave population in the seventeenth century.
- identify the ways Europeans rationalized their involvement in slavery.
- compare the different forms that slavery took in British, French, and Spanish colonies.
- explain how African and European cultures merged in the Americas.

IDENTIFICATIONS

Explain the significance of each of the following:

1. Venture Smith

2. Olaudah Equiano

3. New England Colonies

4. Mid Atlantic Colonies

5. Southern Colonies

6. Sullivan's Island

7. "African knowledge system"

8. rice cultivation

9. Cotton Mather's slave

10. *variolation*

11. saltwater Africans

12. Stono Rebellion

13. New York Rebellion of 1741

14. Fort Mose

15. Menendez

16. Afro-Floridians

17. Afro-Louisianans

18. Samba Bambara

19. manumission

20. *coartacion*

21. Great Awakening

22. Islam

23. Yarrow Mamont

24. Job Ben Solomon

25. Benjamin Lay

26. *juba*

27. trickster spider Anansi

28. Pinkster Day

MULTIPLE CHOICE QUESTIONS

1. This African-born slave was the son of a king who was captured in his village of Anamaboe, Guinea, when he was just eight years old. He was brought to the New England area by way of Barbados and sold into slavery. This proud, defiant, giant of a man had many masters during his 28 years of slavery. He married a willful slave woman and they had three children. He eventually purchased his freedom and painstakingly that of his wife and children. He was focused, determined and dedicated to getting his family and himself out of bondage while standing up for his rights against cruel slave owners. The name he finally settled on was
   A. Olaudah Equiano.
   B. Venture Smith.
   C. Job Ben Solomon.
   D. Samba Bambra.

2. The New England colonies consisted of which of the following groupings?
   A. South Carolina, Georgia, North Carolina, Virginia, Maryland
   B. New Hampshire, Connecticut, Massachusetts, Rhode Island
   C. New York, New Jersey, Pennsylvania, Delaware
   D. Chesapeake Area, Low Country, Tidewater Region, Sea Island Coast

3. The Mid Atlantic or Middle Colonies consisted of which of the following groupings?
   A. South Carolina, Georgia, North Carolina, Virginia, Maryland
   B. New Hampshire, Connecticut, Massachusetts, Rhode Island
   C. New York, New Jersey, Pennsylvania, Delaware
   D. Chesapeake Area, Low Country, Tidewater Region, Sea Island Coast

4. The Southern colonies consisted of which one of the following groupings?
   A. South Carolina, Georgia, North Carolina, Virginia, Maryland
   B. New Hampshire, Connecticut, Massachusetts, Rhode Island
   C. New York, New Jersey, Pennsylvania, Delaware
   D. Chesapeake Area, Low country, Tidewater Region, Sea Island Coast

5. By 1756, slavery functioned differently in various English colonies. Which of the following statements is true?
   A. In the West Indies and in southern ports, colonial societies had made slavery the key to producing goods and services and measuring wealth.
   B. In Philadelphia and other northern ports, slavery was one of many forms of labor and not necessarily a mark of social status for white people.
   C. Almost half of all slaves arriving in the English colonies after 1700 first saw land at Sullivan's Island, a quarantine station in the harbor of Charleston that has been called the Ellis Island of black America.
   D. All of the above.

6. By the early eighteenth century, importation of slaves into the region stretching from Maryland to Georgia doubled. As a result of this growth, it was felt by some planters that all of the following would happen <u>EXCEPT</u>
   A. planters would have to treat their slaves brutally.
   B. numbers make slaves insolent.
   C. slave importation and rice cultivation expanded together.
   D. Virginia legislature would pass a law to limit the numbers of Africans being imported into the colony.

7. "African knowledge system" refers to the fact that
   A. some slaves had planted rice in their homeland and therefore knew much about it.
   B. women in Africa were the ones who had done much of the rice cultivation.
   C. wise planters would allow slaves to impart their knowledge of rice cultivation while foolish planters would not accept any information from a 'lowly slave.'
   D. all of the above.

8. By the early 1700s, many slave ship owners had begun transporting Africans from the west coast of Africa directly to North America, thus bypassing the West Indies. By 1756, the ratio between Africa-born and North American-born slaves had begun to shift in favor of the latter. Which of the following reasons for the transition from African to African American is true?
   A. Large plantations began to edge out small farms and as a result of having large plantations, slaves began living in larger groups.
   B. In large groups, slaves found marriage partners more easily, created families, and built extended kin relationships.
   C. The increase in North American-born slaves gave white planters less reason to import new captives fresh from Africa.
   D. Both B and C are correct.
   E. A, B, and C are correct.

9. Which of the following statements is <u>NOT</u> true?
   A. By the 1770s, Virginia's slave population was expanding at the rate of 5,000 per year, but only about 500 to 800 of them were arriving from Africa.
   B. Most bondsmen and women in the southern colonies labored in the fields.
   C. Slave women worked only in the house as domestic laborers.
   D. Slave women attended the births of the master's children and fed, suckled and bathed his infants.

10. Which of the following statements is <u>NOT</u> true?
   A. Slave women lived under the constant threat of sexual aggression by white men.
   B. Black men often raped white women. When caught, the slave was duly lynched and often decapitated to serve as a warning to other slaves.
   C. In raping black women, white men also asserted their power over black men. In some instances, white slave owners forced black men to witness their assault on a wife, sister or daughter.
   D. The sexual action of white slave owners put their wives in a painful position. The women could only endure silently as their husbands had adulterous relations with their slaves.

11. Which of the following is <u>NOT</u> true about slave life in the North?
   A. North of the Chesapeake, Africans made up only about 5 percent of the population.
   B. Slaves in the North had easier work lives than those in the South, mostly because the northern climate did not permit year-round farming.
   C. African Americans in the North mingled more closely with white people, with white indentured servants, and wage laborers than slaves in the South did.
   D. Black people and Europeans in the North borrowed from and adopted one another's practice of medicine and other knowledge.
   E. All of the above statements are true.

12. What is *variolation*?
   A. A process of curing smallpox
   B. An experiment introduced to white Bostonians by the slave of Cotton Mather that greatly aided the cure of smallpox
   C. The introduction of a small amount of fluid from a smallpox blister under the skin of another person to stimulate the formation of antibodies that gave immunity
   D. All of the above

13. Which group of slaves were the most open in defying their masters?
   A. Newly arrived or saltwater Africans
   B. Female slaves, especially those wishing to free their children
   C. Older slaves who had extensive knowledge of the area and its inhabitants
   D. Teenaged slaves

14. Which of the following was NOT a usual or everyday type of resistance to slavery among slaves?
    A. Working slowly
    B. Destruction of the master's property, theft and lying
    C. Violent resistance
    D. All of the above were common types of rebellion

15. What was the overall result of the New York rebellion and the Stono Rebellion among slaveholders, especially in the South?
    A. Because the revolts were put down successfully, whites felt satisfied with the example they set.
    B. The revolts led to many colonies in the North abolishing slavery, since the whites had been so vicious in beginning the riots against blacks.
    C. The revolts inspired tremendous fear and concern among whites, who attempted to crack down on slaves' opportunities for any type of resistance.
    D. None of the above statements are true.

16. Fort Mose was
    A. the first Free Black town in Colonial North America.
    B. a town for free blacks in Spanish Florida started by Menendez.
    C. all of the above.
    D. A is true, but B is not.

17. What was the Great Awakening?
    A. An idea in America that slaves should rise and overthrow their masters
    B. A large religious revival in the British colonies in the mid to late nineteenth century
    C. An offshoot of The Enlightenment thought which implied that the colonists had a right to overthrow their British masters
    D. All of the above.

18. How was the Christianity of the Great Awakening similar to many native African practices?
    A. The evangelical Protestant ministers' preaching style was similar to African "spirit possession."
    B. The Christian trinity was similar to African beliefs about gods and the creator.
    C. Baptism, as a form of rebirth and renewal, was similar to West African water rituals.
    D. All of the above are true.

19. While some enslaved Africans began to embrace Christianity and blend it with African religious ways, other slaves came as Muslims to North America and continued to practice Islam. Which of the following men were Muslims?

   A. Yarrow Mamout came to America as a slave, became a skilled brickmaker, and eventually obtained his freedom. He lived as a free man for many, many years, became quite wealthy, and was well known around Baltimore. He professed to be 134 years old, which cannot be proven but it is verified that he was at least 100 years old when he died.
   B. Job Ben Solomon arrived in Annapolis, Maryland on a slave ship in 1731. He was sold to a tobacco planter who noticed that Solomon was resistant to field work, but had an agile mind and a princely manner. It was discovered that he was the son of a king in the land of Futa. Before going to London, he was observed writing all of the 6,321 verses of the Koran from memory three times. He eventually returned to his home in Africa and ascended the throne.
   C. Benjamin Lay , an ardent abolitionist, came to the colonies from England with his wife. Because he was a hunchback, Lay felt that he needed to come up with unusual and often times disgusting displays to divulge the horrors of slavery. Lay was easy to ignore because of his eccentricity.
   D. Both A and B are Muslims but not C.
   E. All of the men cited above were Muslims.

20. Which of the following is NOT true about African Americans' cultural influences on whites?

   A. Southerners began to use African-style phrases and intonations in language.
   B. Whites frequently consulted slaves for herbal remedies and other medicines on the plantation.
   C. Whites refused to eat African-style cooking, forcing them to make European-inspired dishes like fried chicken, black-eyed peas and collard greens.
   D. None of the above statements are true.

21. Which English word does not have African roots or origins?

   A. Banjo
   B. Drum
   C. Voodoo
   D. Gumbo

22. Which African instrument survived to be used by slaves on American plantations?

   A. Flute or piccolo
   B. Tambourine
   C. Harpsichord
   D. Banjo

THOUGHT QUESTIONS

1. Acts such as sabotage to the fields, feigning sickness, shamming, and "gold bricking" were used by slaves to resist the institution and to avoid unpaid work. How did slave owners explain such behavior? Why would slave owners be unable or unwilling to recognize these acts as resistance to enslavement?

2. Why do you suppose slaves in colonial North America were treated better in French and Spanish colonies than they were treated in English colonies?

ANSWER KEY MULTIPLE CHOICE QUESTIONS

1 B
2. B
3. C
4. A
5. D
6. D
7. D
8. E
9. C
10. B
11. E
12. D
13. A
14. C
15. C
16. C
17. B
18. D
19. D
20. C
21. B
22. D

CHAPTER 5 *The Revolutionary Era: Crossroads of Freedom*

CHAPTER SUMMARY

Opening Vignette: Thomas Peters Seizes His Freedom

In 1776, Thomas Peters, a slave in Wilmington, North Carolina, faced a hard choice. Amid rumors of slave insurrections, he also heard talk of natural rights that colonists were fighting the British to secure. Should he trust that colonists' talk about natural rights would bring an end to slavery? Or should he flee to the protection of the British? He chose the British—and got both freedom and hardship.

British "Tyranny" and a Cry for Freedom

From 1764 to 1776, white colonists relentlessly proclaimed their love of freedom and their impatience with British oppression—all the while holding black people in slavery. Slave Phillis Wheatley pointed out the contradiction in a book of poems, published in London in 1773; at that time she was one of the most widely read women in North America.

Arguments over taxation and representation mattered little to black Americans, but the language of colonial protest, particularly the idea of inalienable, natural rights, spoke to them. A few white patriots, such as James Otis and Benjamin Rush, recognizing the contradiction between the rhetoric of freedom and the enslavement of Africans, called for an end to slavery. In northern colonies, where slaves had the right to petition, some, such as Prince Hall, petitioned for freedom. In the South, slaves protested and rebelled.

African Americans and the American Revolution

For slaves, the turmoil of wartime opened opportunities for freedom. In 1775, Virginia's governor, Lord Dunmore, promised freedom to those who escaped and joined the British forces. Tens of thousands responded—not only men able to bear arms, but women with children. Some former slaves, such as Peters, fought in British units, but most were consigned to labor. They learned that the British promise of freedom was expedient—little more than a military strategy for recruiting workers and disrupting the economy.

Many free African Americans, and a few slaves, fought for the American cause. Crispus Attucks, killed in the 1770 Boston Massacre, was cited by black historian William C. Nell as the first to lose his life for American independence. Some black patriots were slaves, such as Peter Salem, who fought at Lexington and Bunker Hill, and Washington's slave William Lee. James Armistead, a slave who served as a spy for the Marquis de Lafayette, was emancipated by the Virginia Assembly after the war. Most patriot leaders, however, were reluctant to arm free blacks and slaves until there was a shortage of recruits; in the Deep South neither slave nor free black could serve. But for free blacks such as young James Forten of Philadelphia, wartime service was a chance to demonstrate bravery and commitment to a new nation that they hoped would be dedicated to equality.

Rhetoric and Reality in the New Nation

In the revolutionary era, new state governments and laws grappled with the contradiction between the rhetoric of unalienable rights and reality of slavery. In the South, especially under Methodist influence, antislavery sentiment spread. When Maryland and Virginia lawmakers repealed restrictions on manumissions, the number of free black people soared. But manumissions in the Chesapeake were also due to a decreasing need for slaves, as planters switched from tobacco production to wheat. And at the same time the number of slaves grew through natural increase. In the Lower South, manumission was rare.

North of the Chesapeake, however, slavery was on the road to extinction. Vermont banned slavery from the beginning, and Pennsylvania enacted a gradual emancipation scheme that was adopted by other states as well. Yet slavery was phased out so slowly that there were still 60 slaves in northern states in 1860. In Massachusetts, however, slaves Elizabeth Freeman and Quock Walker sued for their freedom on the basis of the new state constitution that declared "all men are born free and equal." By banning slaveholders from taking slaves into the new territories north of the Ohio River, the Northwest Ordinance of 1787 redefined the future of slavery. While it seemed to restrict its spread, it also allowed slavery in the new territories south of the Ohio.

The Constitutional Settlement

In the new nation, one-fifth of the population was enslaved, and political leaders confronted two problems in considering the abolition of slavery: should owners be compensated for their investment, and could free African Americans fit into American society? The answer to both was no.

The cases of Benjamin Rush and Thomas Jefferson illustrate the contradictions and roadblocks to abolition. Both advocated equality; both owned slaves. But Jefferson, unlike Rush, also held that black people were innately inferior. Though he feared that race mixing would follow emancipation, he had an intimate relationship with his slave Sally Hemings that produced five children. Jefferson's view blinded him to the genius in Phillis Wheatley's poetry and the brilliance of Benjamin Banneker's mathematical calculations. Recognizing the economic and social restrictions imposed on them in the new American republic, some black Americans, such as Prince Hall, promoted plans for a black recolonization of Africa that foreshadowed the black nationalism of later decades.

At the Constitutional Convention in 1787, Gouverneur Morris argued for an end to slavery through compensated emancipation. But northern leaders were unwilling to shoulder this financial responsibility, and delegates from the South, themselves slave owners, declined to discuss the idea, especially after South Carolina and Georgia threatened to withdraw. Consequently, the new Constitution never mentioned slavery but preserved the institution—in the three-fifths clause for calculating representation, in the fugitive slave clause forbidding emancipation of runaways, and in the clause prohibiting Congress from banning the African slave trade for twenty years. While some historians have argued that such compromises were necessary to secure the new nation, others argue that a national abolition plan would have strengthened the union and prevented civil war. Other plans by prominent Virginians for ending slavery went unheeded, though even Jefferson realized that slavery posed a dilemma that would lead to bloodshed.

The Resettlement of African American Loyalists

For those African Americans who had secured freedom by joining the British, American victory meant exile, and Thomas Peters and his family were among those evacuated to Nova Scotia, where British soldiers resettled them on impoverished land. Six years later, Peters and his colleagues petitioned the British government for resettlement elsewhere in the British empire. Peters personally delivered the petition to London, where English abolitionists secured a charter for trade and resettlement rights on the African coast, in Sierra Leone. Returning to Nova Scotia with abolitionist John Clarkson, Peters likened the journey to the exodus of the Israelites out of bondage in Egypt to their homeland. Almost 1,200 former slaves endured the harrowing winter voyage. Their return to Africa was a day of jubilee, but hardships—disease, a shortage of provisions, inept British counselors, racial discord—undermined the new colony. Four months later Peters died and was buried in Freetown, where his descendants live today.

LEARNING OBJECTIVES

Students should be able to

- describe the choices facing slaves on the eve of the American Revolution.
- identify the contradictions between colonists' views of unalienable rights and slavery.
- examine why African Americans joined both the Loyalists and Patriots.
- identify the ways in which the Constitution impacted the status of African Americans.

IDENTIFICATIONS

Explain the significance of each of the following:

1. Thomas Peters

2. Crispus Attucks

3. Phillis Wheatley

4. Nova Scotia

5. Prince Hall

6. Lemuel Haynes

7. Jeremiah Thomas

8. Black Loyalist

9. British Black Guides and Pioneers

10. Colonel Tye

11. Boston King

12. Black Patriots

13. Salem Poor

14. Peter Salem

15. James Armistead

16. William Lee

17. James Otis

18. Lord Dunmore

19. James Forten

20. Elizabeth Freeman

21. Quock Walker

22. Northwest Ordinance

23. Benjamin Rush

24. Sally Hemings

25. Benjamin Banneker

26. Three-Fifths Clause

27. Fugitive Slave Law

28. Sierra Leone

29. compensated emancipation

MULTIPLE CHOICE QUESTIONS

1. Thomas Peters, a Yoruban captured slave, was living on a plantation in Virginia with his wife and child when the Revolutionary War began. His dilemma centered around the side on which to fight- the Patriots or the Loyalists? Which side did he choose and for what reason?
   A. The Patriots because he could identify with their quest for freedom
   B. The Loyalists because they promised freedom for all slaves in the South who would help them defeat the Patriots
   C. The Patriots because they later decided that military help from the slaves was needed and thereby promised freedom to all slaves who would enlist
   D. None of the above statements are correct.

2. This African American was considered by some to be the first American to die during the struggle for independence when he was killed during the Boston Massacre.
   A. Benjamin Banneker
   B. James Forten
   C. Crispus Attucks
   D. Frederick Douglas

3. This African American poet pointed out the contradiction of white colonists who relentlessly proclaimed their love of freedom and their impatience with British oppression yet they held black people in slavery. Her book of poems was published in London in 1773.
   A. Phillis Wheatley
   B. Sojourner Truth
   C. Nikki Giovanni
   D. Harriet Tubman

4. It was in this place that some slaves who fought with the British could find refuge at the end of the war.
   A. Charleston
   B. Nova Scotia
   C. Liberia
   D. Bunker Hill

5. Which of the following noted Americans spoke of the "inalienable, natural rights" of all Americans regardless of color? He called for an end to slavery before the Revolutionary War.
   A. James Otis
   B. Benjamin Rush
   C. Prince Hall
   D. All of the above

6. This son of a white woman and an enslaved African joined the Patriots and fought the British at Boston and Fort Ticonderoga. That same year he wrote a 46 page treatise entitled *"Liberty Further Extended"* wherein he discussed the biblical background to the evils of slavery and the need for total emancipation.
   A. Frederick Douglas
   B. Lemuel Haynes
   C. Olaudah Equiano
   D. David Walker

7. Many slaves in the South joined British ranks in droves. They chose immediate liberty over the uncertainty of being liberated by white Americans voluntarily. They formed such units as the "Ethiopian Regiment" and "Black Guides and Pioneers" and others that were led by white British officers. Which of the following noted African Americans were Black Loyalists?
   A. Thomas Peters
   B. Colonel Tye
   C. Boston King
   D. All of the above

8. Which of the following noted African Americans were Black Patriots?
   A. Salem Poor
   B. Peter Salem
   C. James Armistead
   D. William Lee
   E. All of the above

9. The majority of Black Loyalists was found in the South, while the lesser number of Black Patriots was in the North. This was primarily due to
   A. Southern planters did not offer freedom to the slaves in exchange for military service, but the British did in that area.
   B. Northern slave-owners promised freedom to the slaves in exchange for military service after a shortage of troops became evident.
   C. Northern and Southern whites were afraid to arm black troops.
   D. Both A and B are true, but C is not.
   E. A, B, and C are true.

10. What was true about Lord Dunmore's proclamation in November, 1775?
   A. Since no slave could read, it had little effect on black participation.
   B. Dunmore promised to free slaves who joined the British army.
   C. The proclamation had little effect of any kind on the Americans, who kept very tight control over their slaves.
   D. Dunmore promised that the slaves would be used according to their intellect and leadership abilities.

11. For what is Benjamin Banneker well-known?
   A. His knowledge of chemistry
   B. He was the first black civilian employee of the American government.
   C. He was a well-known minister in the Boston area.
   D. He was a military leader who led black troops into battle during the American Revolution.

12. How did Banneker attempt to change Jefferson's ideas about black people?
   A. He sent a copy of his almanac, and debated racial theories with him.
   B. He became Jefferson's personal secretary, and forced Jefferson to challenge his racist views.
   C. Banneker was so disillusioned with Jefferson that he refused to have anything to do with him.
   D. All of the above.

13. What factors led to the abolition of slavery in the North?
   A. The North's economy was not as dependent on slavery as in the South.
   B. The North was home to Christian ideologies which began to see the injustice in slavery.
   C. Enlightenment rationalism, with its belief in natural rights, was a popular idea.
   D. All of the above.

14. Why did many Quakers take the lead in abolitionism?

A. Quakers had strong African roots.
B. Quaker ideology had long stressed principles of brotherhood of man and nonviolence.
C. Quaker church members served with blacks in the army during the American Revolution, and had seen first-hand their bravery and commitment to liberty.
D. Quakers had never owned slaves, and therefore had no economic interest.

15 . Elizabeth Freeman, popularly known as Mum Bett, is known for all of the following EXCEPT:

A. Serving as a slave in Massachusetts to the Ashley family until Mrs. Ashley hit her with a heated kitchen shovel in 1781.
B. Leaving the Ashley home never to return as a slave and then asking a lawyer to represent her in court in her suit for freedom.
C. For being a hard-working, gentle lady who later served as a midwife and nurse.
D. For posing the intriguing question of whether or not Massachusetts' new state constitution's preamble statement that "all men are born free and equal" applied to her, which Attorney Sedgwick took on as a case to win Freeman's freedom.
E. All of the above

16. Thomas Jefferson often made speeches about the inferiority of the African slave but yet had a long-standing affair with this slave woman with whom he sired five children. She accompanied him to Paris during his tenure as the U.S. Ambassador to France.

A. Sally Heming
B. Dinah Neville
C. Belinda
D. Agnes Studimire

17. Following the war, the British had to dispose of thousands of Black Loyalists who had fled to their camps during the war. Ignoring some whites who suggested the former slaves should be returned to their masters, the British established which of the following sites for Black Loyalists?

A. Nova Scotia in Canada
B. Sierra Leone in West Africa
C. Florida and Jamaica
D. All of the above

18. When drawing up the new Constitution, the words *slave* or *slavery* were not used for fear it would create hostility between northerners and southerners. Which of the following compromises relating to slavery did appear in the document?

    A. Three-fifths Compromise that stated slaves (other persons) would be counted as 3/5s of a person when determining taxation and representation from said State.
    B. A fugitive slave clause forbade the states from emancipating anyone who had fled bondage. The clause also required states to return such runaways to their owners.
    C. A clause prohibited Congress from banning the importation of slaves (called "such persons as any of the states now existing shall think proper to admit") for twenty years.
    D. A and B are true but C is not.
    E. A, B, and C are true.

THOUGHT QUESTIONS

1. How do you suppose the actions of Crispus Attucks during the Boston Massacre may have influenced later black activists?

2. What do the stories of Phillis Wheatley and Benjamin Banneker tell us about African Americans during the period?

3. Why was it possible to abolish slavery in the North, but not in the South?

ANSWER KEY MULTIPLE CHOICE QUESTIONS

1. B
2. C
3. A
4. B
5. D
6. B
7. D
8. E
9. D
10. B
11. B
12. A
13. D
14. B
15. E
16. A
17. D
18. E

CHAPTER 6 *After the Revolution: Constructing Free Life and Combating Slavery, 1787-1816*

CHAPTER SUMMARY

Opening Vignette: Richard Allen and Absalom Jones Lead a Church Walkout

In 1792, preachers Richard Allen and Absalom Jones protested the segregation of black worshipers in St. George's Methodist Church by walking out of services with their followers. The moment was defining: it initiated the formation of independent black churches and indicated the desire of free black communities in the North for respect and equal treatment in the face of growing white hostility.

The Emergence of Free Black Communities

After the Revolution, the number of free blacks grew, from 60,000 in 1790 to more than 233,000 by 1820. Some had purchased their freedom or sued for it in courts; some had escaped slavery or been freed by masters; some were freed when states abolished slavery; and some were new immigrants from the Caribbean. About 40 percent lived in the North and 60 percent in the South, primarily in the Upper South. Most congregated in cities, where they could most readily find friends, marriage partners, and work.

Largely excluded from factory jobs, free black men worked as unskilled laborers and free black women as washerwomen and domestics. Nevertheless, these occupations offered former slaves a sense of dignity and independence. Some free blacks provided services to the black community, with professionals and entrepreneurs forming the nucleus of a tiny middle class. In Philadelphia, James Forten took over a sailmaking enterprise; Richard Allen bought and sold real estate even as he preached and worked at various occupations. Both oversaw large households with relatives and apprentices, but few black families lived so well or independently. Most were impoverished, living as boarders in crowded, crude houses or in attics and cellars. Some free black men chose a life at sea, where black mariners were paid almost the same as white mariners.

In New Orleans, which became part of the United States through the Louisiana Purchase in 1803, the large free black population had a unique culture shaped by years of French and Spanish rule. Two-thirds were mulattos—a middle tier in a hierarchical society, with white people on top and slaves at the bottom. Two-thirds of the city's population was African American.

"Under Our Vine and Fig Tree"

Finding comfort and inspiration in numbers in the cities, African Americans founded their own churches, schools, and community organizations. In Philadelphia, Allen and Jones established the Free African Society, a mutual aid association that used members' dues to assist needy free people.

Jones and Allen believed that black people emerging from slavery needed independent houses of worship. Jones founded the African Church of Philadelphia, and Allen a Methodist church known as Mother Bethel. Black churches arose from a desire for self-government and self-expression, but discrimination in interracial congregations was an additional impetus. White hostility to black independence only intensified, however, as blacks set up churches of their own. The Methodist General Conference sought control over Allen's church until the Pennsylvania Supreme Court affirmed its independence. Mother Bethel was now an African Methodist Episcopal church—a new black denomination. Elsewhere, in Wilmington, Delaware, preacher Peter Spencer had led his followers out of Asbury Methodist to found Ezion Methodist Episcopal, then rejected Methodist control altogether by creating the Union Church of Africans, the first fully autonomous African American church. In their churches, black Christians heard from their preachers that God had not made them inferior; indeed, they were a chosen people, superior to whites mired in the sin of slaveholding. Only in New Orleans, where evangelical Methodism made few inroads, did free blacks not form separate churches. They remained in the Catholic church, which was not segregated.

Black parents also created separate schools for their children. Allen organized the first black Sunday school in America in Philadelphia in 1795. Later, Jones and others established a school for black youth. As in Philadelphia, black schools emerged elsewhere in the country alongside, or within, black churches. Though education was prized, few black families could afford it; most indentured their children at a young age.

Black Revolution in Haiti

Claiming the ideals of the French Revolution as their own, in 1791 the nearly 50,000 free black people on St. Domingue (Haiti) rose up against French royalists. Then the island was plunged into chaos as its 500,000 slaves rose up to claim their freedom. Panicked French planters took their domestic slaves and fled to the American mainland, where their stories of the bloodbath horrified white Americans. A wave of arsons, from Albany to Savannah, intensified fears of a similar slave uprising. For black Americans, however, the revolution in Haiti, led by Toussaint L'Ouverture, was a source of inspiration. When black Haitians defeated European armies to proclaim their independence on January 1, 1804, black Americans rejoiced. Now there was a republic of African people amid the Caribbean slave regimes. Haitian revolutionaries had launched the first anticolonial racial war and achieved the first mass emancipation by slaves.

The revolution in Haiti also inspired black Americans to speak out. When Philadelphia's free blacks—the death-cart drivers and gravediggers—were accused of profiteering during the yellow fever epidemic of 1793, Allen and Jones wrote the first African American attack on slavery after the American Revolution. In *A Narrative of the Proceedings of the Black People, During the Late Awful Calamity,* they cited the slave revolt in Haiti as a warning. In the following years they and others, including Prince Hall, used the right of petition to ask Congress to repudiate the Fugitive Slave Act of 1793, and to ask the nation to live up to the ideals of its founding documents. On January 1, 1808, when American participation in the Atlantic slave trade officially ended, black preachers evoked revolutionary rhetoric in celebration, as this day also marked the birth of the black Haitian republic.

The Spread of Slavery

The banning of the African slave trade did not mean its end, as slave traders continued to smuggle Africans into the Lower South. And the internal slave trade actually increased, as the Louisiana Purchase opened a vast new territory into which slavery could spread. Infusions of northern and southern capital and the invention of the cotton gin accelerated the growth of a new southern economy based on sugar and cotton. Now began a massive transfer of slaves into the lower Mississippi. In Louisiana, where slaves had enjoyed relative freedom under the French and Spanish, Americans added new restrictions, and light-skinned free people of color aligned themselves with white elites.

Slave Resistance

Slaves continued to resist by running away, often hiding in southern swamplands. Increasingly, however, inspired by the Haitian revolution, they rebelled. Gabriel's Rebellion, planned by a young blacksmith in the summer of 1800, aimed to seize Richmond and then demand an end to slavery. A violent storm that washed out the bridges to the city foiled the plan, and a few slaves had leaked news of it to white authorities. Twenty-six conspirators, including Gabriel and his brother Martin, a preacher, were hanged. In court testimony, one of the conspirators compared himself to General Washington, willing to sacrifice his life to secure liberty for his countrymen. Shocked Virginians reacted by tightening restrictions on free blacks. Yet slave plots continued, and in 1811 one of America's largest slave uprisings occurred north of New Orleans, led by a biracial slave from Haiti.

Black Identity in the New Nation

A growing hostility toward free African Americans also led to new restrictions. A naturalization law limited citizenship to white people; state militias limited enlistment to white men. Blacks were prohibited from working for the U.S. postal system and from entering the states of the old Northwest Territory without demonstrating a means of support. And Methodists and Baptists revoked their prohibition of slaveholding among members. Racial conflict was intensified by competition for jobs among the working classes, and it dovetailed with new fears fed by pseudo-scientifically-based racism, which held that differences between races were innate and Africans were immutably inferior.

Thus free African Americans struggled to define their identity in an expanding white nation. For many, Africa was a cultural touchstone, and they called their churches and organizations "African." Freed people took new names, and often their surnames were symbolic, such as Freeman or Newman. Some, despairing of life in the United States, looked to the African homeland. The Free African Society in Newport advocated emigration, as did Paul Cuffe, who hoped also to bring Christianity to Africa.

But Cuffe's back-to-Africa movement was cut short by the War of 1812. As in the Revolution, free black men became soldiers and sailors to prove their allegiance to the new nation, but many slaves—up to 5,000, one-third of them women—joined the British, who again promised freedom. When the British lost, they were exiled, most to Nova Scotia, a few to Sierra Leone.

LEARNING OBJECTIVES

Students should be able to

- identify the factors contributing to the slave rebellion in Saint Domingue and its effects on both white and black Americans.
- describe the characteristics of the growing black communities.
- recognize the ways slaves continued to resist slavery.
- discuss the process and the thinking that free blacks went through in creating their own identity.
- examine the factors contributing to the anti-black racism.
- trace the impact of the Louisiana Purchase on slaves.

IDENTIFICATIONS

Explain the significance of the following:

1. Richard Allen

2. Absalom Jones

3. 1791 slave rebellion in St. Domingue

4. Work life for free blacks

5. James Forten

6. Whaling captain Absalom Boston

7. Family life for free blacks

8. New Orleans: A Unique City

9. mulattoes

10. Black Churches

11. FAS - mutual aid societies

12. Benjamin T. Tanner

13. African American Schools

14. Independent Black Denomination

15. Black Revolution in Haiti

16. *gens de coleur*

17. Toussaint L'Ouverture

18. Reverberations of Haitian rebellion in U.S.

19. Congressional prohibition of Atlantic slave trade - 1808

20. internal or domestic slave trade

21. Louisiana Purchase 1803

22. Napoleon Bonaparte

23. Fugitive Slave Settlements

24. Gabriel's Rebellion

25. Charles Deslondes

26. Rising racial hostility

27. "Double- consciousness"

28. Back-to-Africa movement

29. War of 1812

MULTIPLE CHOICE QUESTIONS

1. Why are Richard Allen and Absalom Jones important in African American history?
   A. They were the first black men to speak for women's rights.
   B. They led the formation of the first separate and independent black churches in America.
   C. They were the first black men elected to the United States Senate.
   D. All of the above are true.

2. In 1792 when Jones and Allen led African American worshippers out of St. George's Methodist Church, in defiance of an attempt to segregate the races during services, it was a momentous occasion. The action led to all of the following EXCEPT:
   A. It initiated the formation of independent black churches.
   B. It indicated the desire of free black communities in the North to supervise their own activities/institutions.
   C. It brought about an end to segregated worship services in all Methodist churches.
   D. All of the above are true.

3. After the Revolution, the number of free blacks grew from 60,000 in 1790 to more than 233,000 in 1820. This was partly due to the fact that
   - A. some free blacks had purchased their freedom.
   - B. some had escaped slavery.
   - C. some had been freed by their masters.
   - D. some were new immigrants from the Caribbean.
   - E. all of the above.

4. Where did most of the free African Americans live?
   - A. 90% of free blacks lived in the North.
   - B. The vast majority of free blacks lived in the Deep or Lower South.
   - C. About 40% lived in the North and 60% lived in the South, primarily in the Upper South.
   - D. 75% of free blacks lived in the North and 25% lived in the South.

5. Most free African Americans congregated in cities where they could most readily find which of the following?
   - A. Friends
   - B. Marriage partners
   - C. Work
   - D. All of the above

6. James Forten and Richard Allen were free African American leaders who were not only affluent but quite involved in all aspects of life for the betterment of African Americans. Which of the following is <u>NOT</u> true?
   - A. Richard Allen was such an honest man that upon finding a trunk with a small fortune in gold and silver, he placed an ad in the newspaper and then refused a reward from the grateful owner. This took place shortly after Allen purchased his freedom in 1779.
   - B. James Forten lived in a three-story home in Philadelphia where he and wife, Charlotte, with their nine children, his deceased sister's four children, an assortment of other relatives, friends, apprentices and borders, presided over a bustling household with various and sundry activities.
   - C. Allen spoke to white audiences about the promising future of free blacks; organized the first black Sunday School in America at Philadelphia in 1795; in 1807 set up a society of free blacks to promote black schools; succeeded in achieving full independence for the African Methodist Episcopal church from the white Conference.
   - D. Forten wrote a fiery article in a Philadelphia newspaper where he attacked, in detail, the racism that was spreading in the city; used his money to support abolitionists causes; maintained a workforce of black and white craftsmen in his thriving sail loft.
   - E. All of the above statements are true.

7. For most urban free black men, jobs in industry were not to be had due to the fact that manufacturers preferred native–born or immigrant whites. The manufacturers erroneously thought that African Americans could not handle the power-driven machinery and were not trainable. Consequently they worked mostly in which of the following unskilled labor jobs?
   A. As stevedores – loading and unloading cargo on the wharves
   B. As cellar-diggers, well-diggers and grave-diggers
   C. As construction laborers and rag pickers
   D. As bootblacks, stablehands, and woodcutters
   E. All of the above

8. Between the years 1787-1816, most urban free black women worked primarily as washerwomen or domestic workers for white families. However every city also had independent black seamstresses, cooks, basket makers, confectioners and street vendors. Which of the following statements would NOT be true of free black women?
   A. Some worked as proprietors of small shops, boardinghouses and oyster cellars.
   B. Many preferred slavery to these new jobs because they had to make too many decisions.
   C. Some African American women worked as midwives, teachers, and nurses.
   D. Many women sold pies, vegetables, fruits, fish, clothing and handmade items from small stands.

9. Of all the black-dominated occupations, seafaring had special importance for free African Americans. Which of the following is NOT a reason for its importance?
   A. Life at sea imposed far less racism on black people than life ashore did.
   B. Ship captains prized any man, regardless of color, who could splice rope properly, haul down canvas quickly in a sudden storm, or scramble aloft to handle the topsails.
   C. Black mariners' pay was equal to that of his white counterparts.
   D. Black mariners quickly became captains because there was hardly any bigotry at sea.
   E. Nearly one out of four mariners sailing out of New York, Philadelphia, Baltimore, New Orleans, and Newport (Rhode Island) was an African American.

10. Family life for free African Americans after the Revolutionary War was affected by which of the following?
   A. Dislocation, which made reuniting families or creating new ones difficult
   B. Family housing, which was difficult to find in cities
   C. The growth of two-parent households in free black communities
   D. All of the above

11. Which of the following is <u>NOT</u> true about New Orleans?

A. Population of free blacks in Louisiana was larger, better established, and more racially mixed than in any other part of the country.
B. By 1810 African Americans represented two-thirds of New Orleans' population of 17,000. Two-thirds of African Americans were free blacks.
C. All African Americans in New Orleans were Catholics.
D. By 1791 nearly two-thirds of all free black people in New Orleans were mulatto.

12. The rise of independent black churches and mutual aid societies, like the FAS, ushered in all of the following feelings <u>EXCEPT:</u>

A. African Americans felt that they could stand on their own as a distinct African people.
B. White Americans resented independent black churches and mutual aid societies. They felt that blacks should remain subservient instead of founding their own organizations.
C. White accusations of black innate inferiority intensified.
D. In their independent churches, black people heard from their own ministers that they were not inferior and that God had made black souls superior to white souls. White people lived in contradiction to their principles of building a democratic republic while maintaining slaves, yet building the republic on slave labor according to the preacher.
E. White people in the North got tired of dealing with free blacks and left them alone.

13. This charismatic Haitian slave led his people in a rebellion against the French and chased the French military forces off the island of St. Domingue.

A. Toussaint L'Ouverture
B. Gabriel
C. Olaudah Equiano
D. Absalom Boston

14. Which of the following statements is <u>NOT</u> true about St. Domingue (now Haiti) before 1791?

A. Half a million Africans toiled on the French-owned western half of the Caribbean island. (Spain controlled the eastern half.) This number nearly matched that in the entire United States.
B. St. Domingue also had about 50,000 *gens de couluer* (free people of color), mostly biracial, who occupied a middle caste.
C. The 32,000 white French colonists – a significant minority – maintained an uncertain grip on power.
D. American whites had no interest in the affairs of slaves in St. Domingue.

15. What effects did the Haitian Revolution have on Americans?

    A. It dismayed white Americans when French planters and merchants from the island brought their slaves with them to the U.S. The lurid stories of the blood baths in Haiti frightened white Americans.
    B. Whites were afraid that the fever of black rebellion would spread throughout the U.S.
    C. Many black Americans lauded the slave rebellion and began to look upon the possibility of being participants in a hemisphere-wide offensive against slavery.
    D. Black Americans marveled at how Haiti's half-million slaves defeated the combined might of French, English, and Spanish armies intent on reshackling them.
    E. All of the above.

16. The congressional prohibition of the Atlantic slave trade, to become effective in 1808, did not eradicate traffic in human beings. Many southern congressmen who had agreed to the ban did not do so for humanitarian reasons but because rapid natural increase among slaves made new importations unnecessary in their states.
Slavery actually expanded after 1808 due to all of the following <u>EXCEPT</u>

    A. Slave traders in the Lower South, in defiance of the law, continued to import slaves.
    B. The internal slave trade -the selling of human property from region to region within the United States- actually intensified.
    C. The Three-Fifths Compromise came into play.
    D. The slave birth rate exceeded the death rate.

17. What was the most common form of resistance to slavery among blacks?

    A. Physical violence against the white masters
    B. Poisoning of whites by slave cooks
    C. Day-to-day resistance and even escape
    D. None of the above were common.

18. Gabriel (Prosser) planned a slave insurrection in Virginia that never took place; however he and other alleged conspirators were hanged for the plot. Which of the following was <u>NOT</u> an effect of Gabriel's Rebellion?

    A. Fearing for their lives, more whites began to liberate their slaves.
    B. Gabriel's network continued to exist and be influential after his death.
    C. His message of liberation was spread westward with the slave trade.
    D. All of the above.

19. Who organized the Louisiana Rebellion?

    A. Gabriel (Prosser)
    B. (Charles) Deslondes
    C. Nat Turner
    D. John Brown

20. Which of the following statements is <u>true</u> about the Southern reaction to slave violence?
    A. They decided to enact laws and practices to make slavery harsher.
    B. Fear and concern swept the South.
    C. They began to be much more suspicious of foreigners and outsiders, including Northerners.
    D. All of the above are true.

21. The term "double-consciousness," as penned by the famous African American historian W.E.B. Du Bois, describes all of the following statements about free blacks <u>EXCEPT:</u>
    A. Free blacks were often torn with their identity as *African* Americans. Should their allegiance be tied to a land they knew little of? But yet they continued many of the traditions of the motherland.
    B. Were newly freed people *African* Americans? Did their future lie where they had toiled most of their lives? Or were they simply Americans with dark skin?
    C. Should they regard themselves as Africans living in a strange hostile land or as a displaced people who might do best to return to the realms of their ancestors?
    D. The African half of this double-consciousness showed itself plainly in the way freed slaves named their organizations and churches. In adopting new names, most recently freed slaves disposed of their slave names altogether.
    E. All of the above statements are true.

THOUGHT QUESTIONS

1. Why did separate black churches and other institutions emerge during this period? How does this compare to the overall theme of integration during the Civil Rights Movement of the twentieth century?

2. How did free blacks see themselves? Did they actually want to assimilate into the mainstream of American life, or did they want to maintain their own distinct culture? Why?

ANSWER KEY MULTIPLE CHOICE QUESTIONS

1. B
2. C
3. E
4. C
5. D
6. E
7. E
8. B
9. D
10. D
11. C
12. E
13. A
14. D
15. E
16. C
17. C
18. A
19. B
20. D
21. E

CHAPTER 7 *African Americans in the Antebellum Era*

CHAPTER SUMMARY

Opening Vignette: James Forten on Repatriation to Africa

In 1817, James Forten laid a choice before free black men at Philadelphia's Mother Bethel church: would they favor, or oppose, returning to ancestral Africa. Unanimously, they opposed, perceiving colonization as a white scheme to make slaveholding more secure. It was a defining moment, for it linked the lives of free blacks to freedom for slaves.

Black Religion in the Antebellum Era

As white hostility intensified, the number of separate black churches increased. In 1816, black Methodist congregations joined to found the African Methodist Episcopal (AME) Church as a separate denomination, naming Richard Allen as its first bishop. In his own congregation, Allen faced a dilemma when Jarena Lee claimed God had commanded her to preach, as Methodism had no provision for women preachers. But Lee, a charismatic, persisted, eventually preaching not only at Allen's pulpit but across the country, inspiring AME women to church work and to fully use their spiritual gifts.

The Expansion of Slavery

The invention of the cotton gin in 1793, which mechanically removed the sticky seeds from the fibers, made cotton production efficient just as the Louisiana Purchase was making new lands in the south and west available for cotton cultivation. Soon cotton was an engine of economic development, as southern planters cleared new cotton fields in the Old Southwest, and New England textile factories turned cotton fibers into coveted cloth.

But as cotton production increased, so did the slave population and the internal slave trade. Manumissions declined, as masters sold their slaves south. Some 800,000 African Americans—about one-third of all slaves aged eighteen to thirty—were sent on a new forced migration that shattered slave families and separated kinfolk as never before. Marched overland or shipped by sea, slaves cleared and cultivated new lands in the Old Southwest (some of which was later vacated by the expulsion of Native Americans) and Louisiana Territory. By the time Mississippi and Alabama were admitted to the union as states in 1817 and 1819, their slaves were producing half the nation's cotton.

Soon cotton cultivation spread west of the Mississippi River, and in 1819, when Missouri Territory applied for statehood with guarantees of slaveholding, Congress was forced to face the issue of slavery in the territories. The balance of slave and free states was preserved in a compromise that admitted Maine and drew a line that divided the rest of Louisiana Territory into future slave and free states. But when Missouri's constitution forbade the entry of free black Americans into the new state, Congress faced an additional issue: black citizenship. Some northerners argued that free blacks had constitutional rights, while some southerners pointed out that northern states denied them these rights. In the end, the term *citizen* was left undefined and Missouri was left to pass its own laws. Though the Missouri Compromise temporarily shelved the issue of slavery's expansion and free blacks' rights, the debates had made slavery a national flashpoint, preoccupying the country's leaders and heightening sectional tensions.

Slave Life and Labor

Succinctly expressed by Frederick Douglass, the essence of slave life was the expropriation of labor. Slave labor took many forms depending on the region and the crop: life was easier in the wheat and tobacco fields of the Upper South than in the swampy rice and indigo fields of coastal Carolina and Georgia; it was easier for those who worked as artisans and domestics than for field hands. But on the eve of the Civil War, three-quarters of all slaves worked in the cotton fields, driven by the lash. Slave women were worked as hard in the fields as men; they also managed domestic duties in their quarters and were also subjected to frequent sexual abuse by white masters.

In southern cities, where about one-tenth of all slaves and at least one-third of free black people lived, work regimens had greater variety than on plantations. Many slaves became artisans and, in contrast to the North, were increasingly used in industry as factory owners sought to eliminate the threat of strikes. Some masters leased slaves, and some slaves undertook self-hiring, making their own contracts for work. While this practice gave them some degree of control and hopes for self-purchase, it also placed them in direct competition with white laborers.

Regardless of type of work, slaves knew that masters held arbitrary power over them. Some masters, especially in the Upper South, adopted a paternalistic approach, arguing that the slave system involved mutual obligation, even a Christian stewardship. But for most, the slave system was held in place by physical, psychological, and legal cruelty, evidenced in whipping, sexual assault, and the threat of auction. Yet daily interactions between black and white people ensured the continuing exchange of cultural practices.

Sundown to Sunup: Slaves on Their Own Time

Though their labor was expropriated, slaves nourished their souls and maintained their human dignity through family and religion. Masters encouraged childbearing, as each birth constituted a capital gain, but auctions brought the agony of separation. Slave women had none of the protections white women enjoyed; the domestic ideal—in which women were supposed to make the home a haven—had no meaning for them. Yet despite obstacles, slave men and women made marriage commitments and maintained family connections; slave children sold away from their families gained fictive aunts and uncles. Elders prepared children for a cruel world and taught them how to survive in it.

Spirituality was the second source of support and solace. Adapting African supernatural ideas and spiritual ways to Christianity, slaves seized on the stories of Moses leading his people out of bondage and of David overcoming the giant Goliath. In southern cities, African Methodist and African Baptist churches grew rapidly. Male preachers played key roles, but women outnumbered men. Black religious and secular agendas overlapped in songs, music, and dance, which gave sustenance and the promise of hope and freedom.

Resistance and Rebellion

Increasingly, free and enslaved African Americans found a call to arms in religion. Inspired by the evangelicalism of the Second Great Awakening, black churches became centers of resistance to slavery. In 1822 in Charleston, Denmark Vesey, a free, literate, wealthy black Methodist leader planned a slave rebellion inspired by the Haitian Revolution and promoted in biblical terms. Betrayed, the plotters were executed. The magistrate who sentenced Vesey to death could not understand why a free man should have risked his comfortable life. As with earlier slave conspiracies, authorities stiffened restrictions on blacks in Charleston and razed its AME church.

In 1829, another free black, David Walker, published *An Appeal to the Coloured Citizens of the World*, which challenged free African Americans to see themselves as part of a worldwide movement for freedom and to regard armed struggle against slaveholders as divinely sanctioned. Grounded in Scripture, Walker's messianic advocacy of rebellion was provocative and prophetic. The year after Walker died, in 1830, William Lloyd Garrison's *Liberator* began its relentless call for an immediate end to slavery.

Then in 1831, Nat Turner, a slave in Southampton County, Virginia, interpreted a solar eclipse as God's call to rebellion. With sixty slaves, he slew fifty-five white men, women, and children before the uprising was put down by the militia. About to be executed, Turner related his "confessions," which stunned white southerners in his messianic claim that slavery would destroy the nation. Frightened Virginians debated abolishing slavery but instead passed new laws prohibiting whites from teaching slaves to read or write and blacks from preaching Christianity. Yet African Americans found inspiration in Turner's visionary quest for liberation and Christian challenge to the sin of slaveholding.

Free Black Organizing

By 1830, black leaders in northern cities began to organize and coordinate resistance to colonization, the expansion of slavery, and discrimination. New black newspapers helped provide a forum and create an urban-based network. Following a race riot in Cincinnati, black leaders met in Philadelphia to form the American Society of Free People of Color, under Allen's leadership. A second convention met the following year.

Even as worldwide sentiment was turning sharply against slavery, slaveholders in America were strengthening their grip on the nation's economy and political system. Andrew Jackson was the fifth slave-owning president, and Vice President John C. Calhoun was promoting a theory called nullification. Evoked as a state means of countering the effect of a federal tariff, it was clearly intended to protect slavery against federal action in a nation that was increasingly divided.

LEARNING OBJECTIVES

Students should be able to

- identify the ways in which free and enslaved African Americans challenged slavery.
- describe the relationship between the expansion of cotton cultivation and the growth of slavery.
- examine the lives that slaves forged on plantations.
- discuss the importance of the church within the black community.
- explain how slavery became more entrenched during this era.

IDENTIFICATIONS

Explain the significance of each of the following:

1. Antebellum
2. Repatriation
3. American Colonization Society (ACS)
4. James Forten
5. Richard Allen
6. Missouri Compromise
7. Denmark Vesey
8. Absalom Jones
9. Paul Cuffe
10. David Walker
11. William Lloyd Garrison
12. Nat Turner
13. *Life and Religious Experience of Jarena Lee*
14. Eli Whitney
15. Internal or Domestic Slave Trade
16. Frederick Douglass
17. Solomon Northrup

18. Gabriel

19. Morris Brown

MULTIPLE CHOICE QUESTIONS

1. Many free African Americans were opposed to the repatriation proposed by James Forten, Paul Coffe and others for the following reason:
   A. They were afraid that all free blacks would be forced to go.
   B. They did not believe that whites wanted to do "a great good" for people they hated.
   C. They felt certain that "the slaveholders wanted to get rid of free blacks so as to make their slave property more secure."
   D. All of the above.

2. Of the following groupings of noted African Americans, which grouping consists of insurrectionists?
   A. Frederick Douglass, Absalom Jones, Richard Allen
   B. Gabriel, Denmark Vesey, Nat Turner
   C. Solomon Northrup, Morris Brown, Harriet Tubman
   D. Sojourner Truth, Benjamin Banneker, Prince Hall

3. The Antebellum Era refers to
   A. the years directly following the Revolutionary War (1781 – 1808).
   B. the years following the Civil War (1865 -1890).
   C. that period of time, roughly forty years, before the Civil War (1820-1860).
   D. those years, roughly forty years, preceding the Revolutionary War (1735-1775).

4. This institution served as the rock on which all black struggles for freedom and equality rested.
   A. Mutual aid societies
   B. Black independent church
   C. Black families
   D. Underground Railroad

5. Charismatic preachers attracted large numbers of African Americans during the Antebellum Era. Of the following charismatic preachers, which one was NOT allowed to take to the pulpit in the AME church?
   A. Richard Allen
   B. Absalom Jones
   C. Jarena Lee
   D. Sojourner Truth

6. Which of the following issues came about as a by-product of the invention of the cotton gin?
   A. Land in the Deep/Lower South was ripe for planting cotton.
   B. Native Americans were forced to move west of the Mississippi River.
   C. Slave manumissions decreased.
   D. All of the above.

7. The inventor of the cotton gin was
   A. Cyrus McCormick.
   B. Eli Whitney.
   C. John Deere.
   D. Alexander Graham Bell.

8. As a result of the invention of the cotton gin in 1793, which of the following is NOT true?
   A. Slave coffles trudged south from Virginia, Maryland, Delaware, and North Carolina.
   B. The sharp rise in cotton production marked a turning point for the South and the nation.
   C. 800,000 slaves were emancipated.
   D. Slave families were broken up as thousands of slaves, age 18 to 30, were sent farther south and west.

9. Which of the following provisions is NOT a part of the Missouri Compromise?
   A. Maine would be admitted as a free state, while Missouri would come into the Union as a slave state.
   B. From that time on, all territory that was part of the Louisiana Purchase north of the 36" 30' would come in as free states, and that territory south of the line could become slave states.
   C. The slave trade, but not slavery itself, should be abolished in Washington, D.C.
   D. All of the above are true.

10. This African American was born free in New York, where he lived with his wife and children until 1841. After being captured in D.C. and sold into slavery in the Lower South, he lived as a slave and wrote a book *Twelve Years a Slave* after escaping. This man was
   A. Solomon Northrup.
   B. Frederick Douglass.
   C. Prince Hall.
   D. James Forten.

11. Slaves worked in all of the following arenas EXCEPT
   A. agriculture as field hands.
   B. domestic work as house servants.
   C. cities as skilled laborers.
   D. industry as workers in manufacturing plants.
   E. All of the above are true.

12. In order to find meaning and some joy in his/her dismal lives, slaves often took refuge in which of the following?
    A. Religion and family
    B. Sabotaging the fields
    C. Working hard for the master
    D. Dreams of returning to Africa

13. This free African American risked his freedom to plan a slave insurrection in Charleston in 1822 because he felt it was the right thing to do and that it was biblical. The plot was discovered; he was tried and executed. The wealthy black Methodist leader was
    A. Denmark Vesey.
    B. Gabriel.
    C. Nat Turner.
    D. Charles Deslondes.

14. This free African American published *An Appeal to the Coloured Citizens of the World*, as a challenge to free blacks and to slaves to arm themselves and kill whites if necessary in order to bring about abolition of slavery. He died mysteriously a year after his book was published. The person in question is
    A. Nat Turner.
    B. David Walker.
    C. Denmark Vesey.
    D. Charles Deslondes.

15. This literate, self taught slave from Southampton, Virginia, planned and executed a slave rebellion in 1831 whereby 60 armed slaves killed 55 white men, women and children before the rebellion was crushed. For this crime he, along with fellow conspirators, was executed and hundreds more African Americans were put to death when suspected to be part of the rebellion. The slave leader was
    A. Nat Turner.
    B. David Walker.
    C. Denmark Vesey.
    D. Charles Deslondes.

THOUGHT QUESTIONS

1. What common threads appear in the character of courageous African American leaders like Denmark Vesey, David Walker or Nat Turner? Do you think you could challenge an unfair governmental policy in the twenty-first Century?

2. A single innovation entrenched slavery in America just as European nations and the new South American republics were abolishing slavery. What was it and what effect did it have on slavery and the southern economy?

ANSWER KEY MULTIPLE CHOICE QUESTIONS

1. D
2. B
3. C
4. B
5. D
6. D.
7. B
8. C
9. C
10. A
11. E
12. A
13. A
14. B
15. A

CHAPTER 8 *African Americans in the Reform Era 1831-1850*

CHAPTER SUMMARY

Opening Vignette: James Forten Advocates an Immediate End to Slavery

In 1830, James Forten wrote to William Lloyd Garrison, "We are not treated as freemen, in any part of the United States." Yet he would not leave America for Africa. In the reformist spirit of the era, he resolved to work for abolition, believing that toppling the slave regime would end racial hostility. When Garrison published his first issue of *The Liberator,* it included an article by Forten titled "Men Must Be Free."

Black Americans in an Expanding Nation

In the South, the slave population grew by 25 percent every decade from 1820 to 1860, primarily through natural increase. Illegal importation of slaves continued, while manumissions declined. In the North, the number of free blacks grew so slowly that the proportion of the African American population dropped. In the cities, both enslaved and free women outnumbered men, making family formation difficult.

Free African Americans preferred cities, and New York and Philadelphia became thriving centers of black religious and intellectual life. Across the North, such communities were tightly knit around black churches. Some separate black communities also emerged in the South, a few sponsored by philanthropic white people. And some free people chose to settle in separate communities on the frontiers.

In 1839, black leader Martin Delany toured the United States, encountering a variety of lifestyles among free and enslaved blacks. Some black people mixed with native populations, as in Florida, where John Horse, part African American, part Creek, joined in wars against federal policy that would remove the Seminoles to Indian territory. A few slaves, such as Benjamin Montgomery in Mississippi, secured unusual privileges. Literate, he read books from his master's library and engaged in surveying and mechanical projects.

Colored Americans and Reform

Influenced by the evangelicalism of the Great Awakening, black Americans like Maria Stewart of Boston hoped to cleanse the country of sin. Stewart argued that citizenship could be earned through thrift and sobriety and that discrimination against women prevented advancement and mocked Christian virtue. Though the first female public speaker in America whose speeches were published, she encountered hostility and withdrew from public life.

Yet Stewart's message of self-improvement resonated in black communities. In Pittsburgh, Lewis Woodson argued that literacy was necessary for productive citizenship, and in Philadelphia, Forten presided over the American Moral Reform Society, committed to "education, temperance, economy, and universal liberty." Dozens of black organizations modeled responsible citizenship by providing musical, recreational, and burial services, but most vital was education. As public schools excluded black students, dedicated teachers founded separate schools for them. Black people reinforced their American identity by abandoning the designation "African" for "colored."

The Abolitionist Movement

The founding of the American Anti-Slavery Society (AAS) in Philadelphia in 1833 announced the arrival of a radical abolitionism, with reformers prepared to break laws, confront slaveholders, and even commit violence. Much leadership for the abolitionist movement came from black churches, but white organizers such as Garrison and Lydia Maria Child lectured on the immorality of slavery and promoted abolitionist ideas through books, articles, and newspapers such as *The Liberator.* A particularly effective writer and lecturer was Frederick Douglass, who escaped from slavery in 1838. Abolitionists also aided fugitive slaves, wrote antislavery petitions, and boycotted products made with slave labor. The American Missionary Association (AMA) urged members to refrain from business with slaveholders. From black communities came antislavery newssheets such as Russwurm and Cornish's *Freedom's Journal,* Delany's *Mystery,* and Douglass's *North Star,* launched with Delany and William C. Nell.

But though abolitionists agreed on the goal of ending slavery, they differed in methods and motivations. Arthur and Lewis Tappan worried that slavery compromised white Americans' morality; Garrison sought immediate abolition but sought also to control black abolitionists, as did Child; Gerrit Smith donated land for a black community and, later, helped fund John Brown's raid. The AMA sought to cleanse Americans of the sin of slavery—and to rid America of black people by sending them to Liberia. Even among free black Americans there were divisions, and some only gradually conceived of their fate as intertwined with that of slaves. Gender was another source of division, as some groups prohibited women members and some women formed their own organizations. Abbey Kelley's appointment to the AAS executive committee in 1840 split the organization.

The AAS's confrontational posture incited violence among northerners as well as southerners. A white mob fearing black labor competition almost killed Garrison in Boston, and in Alston, Illinois, a white mob murdered Elijah Lovejoy, publisher of an abolitionist newspaper. In Philadelphia, a mob burned down a meeting hall built by abolitionists the day after its inaugural lecture. Between 1833 and 1838, more than three dozen race riots in northern cities targeted symbols of black independence—churches, businesses, meeting places, and prosperous black families. In the South, abolitionism dissolved in the wake of Nat Turner's rebellion, and those who favored the end of slavery, such as James Birney and the Grimké sisters, quietly left the region.

Following the Missouri Compromise, tension about slavery underlay every debate in Congress, especially as the burgeoning population of the northern states foretold the decline of slaveholders' power. In 1836, Congress instituted the Gag Rule, prohibiting the reading or discussion of antislavery petitions. Legal cases surrounding slave revolts on the slave ships *Amistad* and *Creole* set precedents for court attention to abolitionism.

Limitations and Opportunities

Growing restrictions on free African Americans in the South and new laws denying them the vote in the North made it clear that abolitionist agitation was not enough. Even the new Liberty Party, nominating Birney for president in 1840, offered little hope for a political solution. But it underscored the irony of black leaders like Douglass and Delany supporting a candidate for whom most black people could not vote.

Some black Americans sought freeman's rights on western frontiers, especially after the discovery of gold in California. But the slavery issue and racial discrimination accompanied American expansion. After Mexico achieved independence from Spain in 1821 and abolished slavery, Texas became pivotal to U.S. politics. Texans wanting to maintain slavery broke from Mexico in 1836, and when, after a period of independence, they sought entry into the union as a slave state, abolitionists objected. A subsequent war with Mexico over Texas had profound consequences, opening new territories to slavery and a bitter debate in Congress over the issue. The Compromise of 1850 contained four momentous provisions. California was admitted as a free state, for the first time tilting the balance in the Senate. Settlers in New Mexico and Utah would eventually decide whether their states would be slave or free. The slave trade (but not slavery) was abolished in the District of Columbia. And a new Fugitive Slave Act denied fugitives a jury trial and compelled citizens to help apprehend them. Intended to be the "final settlement" of the slavery question, the compromise actually brought to nation closer to crisis.

LEARNING OBJECTIVES

Students should be able to

- analyze the increasing tensions between free blacks and whites.
- describe the westward expansion of Americans, both black and white.
- discuss the various reform efforts led by African Americans.
- identify the ideas of prominent abolitionists.

IDENTIFICATIONS

Explain the significance of each of the following:

1. James Forten

2. William Lloyd Garrison

3. abolitionists

4. Martin Delaney

5. manumission

6. John Horse or John Caballo

7. Osceola

8. Andrew Jackson

9. Indian Removal Act

10. Benjamin Thornton Montgomery

11. Maria Miller Stewart

12. Ira Alridge

13. Daniel Payne

14. Frederick Douglass

15. *The Liberator*

16. *The North Star*

17. AAS

18. AME Church

19. Lewis Tappan

20. James Curry

21. Robert Purvis

22. Henry Highland Garnett

23. Lucretia Mott

24. Elijah Lovejoy

25. *Drapetomania*

26. Gag Rule

27. *Amistad*

28. Sengbe Pieh or Joseph Cinque

29. Lone Star Republic

30. Mexican American War

31. Treaty of Guadaloupe Hidalgo

32. James Beckwourth

33. Missouri Compromise- 1820

34. Compromise of 1850

35. *Creole*

MULTIPLE CHOICE QUESTIONS

1. An abolitionist is one who favored
    A. keeping slavery where it was.
    B. keeping slavery from spreading to new territory.
    C. abolishing slavery in all states and territories.
    D. emancipating slaves in the Lower South only.

2. Of the following abolitionists, which one was white?
    A. William Lloyd Garrison
    B. Frederick Douglass
    C. James Forten
    D. Robert Purvis

3. How did William Lloyd Garrison change the nature of the anti-slavery movement?
    A. He attempted to exclude women from the anti-slavery movement.
    B. He thought that whites should play the main role, and refused to allow any black membership in his organization.
    C. He called for the immediate abolition of slavery, along with a commitment to racial justice.
    D. He called for violent uprisings and the murder of slaveholders.

4. What were some of the problems the anti-slavery movement encountered in its interracial efforts?
    A. Whites refused to allow blacks to have equal status in the organizations, despite their language of equality and justice.
    B. Anti-slavery organizations were actually very well integrated, and allowed blacks huge levels of power.
    C. The anti-slavery movement was completely white, and was never an interracial effort.
    D. None of the above.

5. The African American population jumped from 2.3 million in 1830 to 3.6 million in 1850. The largest percentage of growth came from the slave population. Free black population dwindled by 2 percent. What accounts for those figures?
    A. There was less manumission by slave-owners.
    B. The high fertility rates of enslaved women swelled the slave population. The average slave woman bore seven children.
    C. Slave birth rate was higher than the death rate.
    D. All of the above.

6. This African American was born in 1812, studied in a black church school, and subsequently worked as a barber and a cupper and leecher (a medical practitioner who treated illness by drawing blood from the patient). He was an ardent abolitionist and a restless man who eventually traveled throughout the country observing slave conditions and abolitionists' activities.
   A. Robert Purvis
   B. Martin Delaney
   C. Elijah Lovejoy
   D. James Beckwourth

7. This African American was part Native American. His mother was probably a black slave woman who had a child by her Seminole master. He fought with the Seminoles against U.S. troops in the First Seminole War that began in 1835 and continued for five years. The Seminoles were fighting in resistance to the Indian Removal Act. By 1840 he had married a Seminole woman and he eventually changed sides and served with U.S. troops as a guide and interpreter and later as a soldier. He straddled the fence between being black or Indian and between slave or free. Who was he?
   A. John Horse
   B. Osceola
   C. Geronimo
   D. Cochise

8. What were the goals of the American Anti-Slavery Society?
   A. To restrict slavery to the South where it already existed
   B. The immediate end to slavery, with no compensation for owners
   C. The gradual end to slavery, with some compensation to owners for their losses
   D. The immediate end to slavery with compensation for owners

9. This slave managed to carve out a degree of freedom while being enslaved and eventually purchased his wife's freedom but not his own. His master was one of the few slave-owners who recognized the economic principle of providing the best working environment in order to get the most productivity from the workers. Based on this principle, this literate slave worked on the Hurricane Plantation in Mississippi, mastered surveying, drafting and mechanical skills and supervised construction work on the plantation.
   A. Ira Alridge
   B. Daniel Payne
   C. Benjamin Thornton Montgomery
   D. Lewis Tappan

10. Building on the reform spirit, free African Americans sought to gain skills and resources to shield themselves from racism and exploitation. They established schools and literary societies for both children and adults. They boycotted slave-produced goods to protest slavery. Black ministers preached about humility and patience. Some also taught rebellion. Which of the following free African Americans distinguished themselves by participating in the reform movement in such a manner?
    A. Maria Miller Stewart
    B. Ira Alridge
    C. Daniel Payne
    D. All of the above.

11. Free African Americans enjoyed a luxury unavailable to most slaves: choosing their children's names. Which of the following concerns did <u>NOT</u> have an effect on the names chosen?
    A. Parents chose biblical names.
    B. Newly freed blacks chose names that exemplified their new status such as Freeman, Newman, Trusty, etc.
    C. Some chose names connected with their former beloved slave masters.
    D. Some chose names that reflected black history or literature, such as Toussaint L'Ouverture Delany or Alexander Dumas Delany.
    E. Reform-era black names often bespoke knowledge of literature, history, and current events stretching far beyond the limits of a slave world.

12. This outstanding African American was an escaped slave whose freedom Philadelphia abolitionists purchased. He served as an apprentice/mentee to William Lloyd Garrison. He is more noted for his oratory ability and his dedication to the abolitionist cause. He also became editor/ publisher of *The North Star*.
    A. David Walker
    B. Nat Turner
    C. Frederick Douglass
    D. James Forten

13. This African American church had the largest following during the period 1831-1850.
    A. AME
    B. Baptist
    C. Catholic
    D. Presbyterian

14. Which of the following are <u>NOT</u> correctly linked or paired?
    A. Robert Purvis, Henry Highland Garnett—Black members of AAS
    B. Mexican American War, Treaty of Guadalupe Hidalgo—1846-1848
    C. Joseph Cinque, *Amistad*—Slave rebellion in the Atlantic
    D. Lucretia Mott, Elijah Lovejoy—White members of AAS
    E. Gag Rule, *drapetomania* —Congressional measures related to slavery

15. Both the Missouri Compromise (1820) and the Compromise of 1850 had provisions that affected the spread of slavery. Which of the following is true?

    A. The Missouri Compromise stated that in all territory that had been part of the Louisiana Purchase, slavery would be forbidden north of the 36 degrees and 30 minutes line.
    B. The Compromise of 1850 stated that California would be admitted as a free state, but in the remainder of the territory acquired from Mexico, popular sovereignty would decide the slave question.
    C. In the Missouri Compromise, Maine would be admitted to the Union as a free state while Missouri could come in as a slave state in 1820, thereby maintaining the balance of free states and slave states.
    D. In the Compromise of 1850 the slave trade, but not slavery itself, was abolished in Washington, D.C.
    E. All of the above.

THOUGHT QUESTIONS

1. Some abolitionists viewed slavery as being immoral. How was religion used to critique slavery? How was religion used to justify slavery?

2. How did the strategies or actions of white abolitionists differ from those of black abolitionists? How were they similar?

ANSWER KEY MULTIPLE CHOICE QUESTIONS

1. C
2. A
3. C
4. A
5. D
6. B
7. A
8. B
9. C
10. D
11. C
12. C
13. A
14. E
15. E

CHAPTER 9 *A Prelude to War: The 1850s*

CHAPTER SUMMARY

Opening Vignette: Tragedy and Triumph at Christiana

A pitched battled at Christiana, Pennsylvania, in September 1851, dramatized the regional and racial tensions tearing American society apart. A Maryland slaveowner had come to reclaim his property—several young male slaves who had escaped the previous year. But they stood their ground, supported by others in the black community and by white antislavery Quakers, who broke the law by refusing to help the slave-hunters. In the fray, the black men prevailed and the slaveowner was killed, and in the trials that followed, the white resisters were acquitted.

Conflict over the Fugitive Slave Act of 1850

The Fugitive Slave Act, which strengthened federal control of the apprehension of runaways, raised tensions over federal versus state power, over property rights, and between regions, increasing the gulf dividing the industrializing North and the plantation South. The Constitution and federal laws had protected the property rights of slaveholders by requiring the return of fugitives, and the new law required citizens to assist, under penalty of treason. But northern states had passed personal liberty laws prohibiting state officials from aiding slave-catchers, and Massachusetts boldly nullified the new law. Across the North many without strong abolitionist sympathies now resisted federal marshals on principle. The new law also meant that fugitives had to leave the country to be secure. Northern reformers feared a "slavocracy;" southerners feared a loss of property.

Meanwhile, the Fugitive Slave Act intensified slaves' desperation, and growing numbers, probably 75,000 in the 1850s, escaped along a network known as the Underground Railroad. Harriet Tubman was the most famous "conductor," and slaveholders feared the new posture of black defiance that she represented. Other conductors included William Still, a black Philadelphian, and Levi Coffin, a white Quaker from North Carolina.

The experience of Anthony Burns exemplifies how the Fugitive Slave Act played out in the North. When Burns, an escaped slave working in Boston, was arrested, angry white and black abolitionists stormed the courthouse. On trial was southerners' constitutional right to federal protection of their property. Burns was returned to his owner, but his trial invigorated abolitionists, such as Charlotte Forten, and new efforts in fund-raising and petitioning. Eventually the Boston Vigilance Committee purchased Burns's freedom.

The Power of Stories

In this decade, long silenced black Americans finally had a voice. In slave narratives, escaped slaves such as Frederick Douglass revealed the abuses of the slave system. Henry "Box" Brown wrote a dramatic account of how he shipped himself in a box from Richmond to Philadelphia, and on the lecture circuit William and Ellen Craft related the disguises they used in their escape.

Isabella Van Wageren took the new name of Sojourner Truth, dictating her life story and lecturing on the evils of slavery and the oppression of women. Harriet Jacobs revealed sexual abuse by slave owners, and Harriet Wilson described the abuse free black women endured. The historical writings of William C. Nell, the fiction of William Wells, and the poetry of Francis Ellen Watkins revealed black Americans as complex human beings. Watkins also challenged: “Could slavery exist long if it did not sit on a commercial throne?”

White Americans too, used stories of slavery’s horror to advance the antislavery cause, including an incident in which Margaret Garner killed her children rather than see them seized back into slavery. Harriet Beecher Stowe’s *Uncle Tom’s Cabin,* a romanticized version of slavery, captured the sympathies of many who had not previously advocated abolition. Annoyed that Stowe’s hero was so passive about bondage, Martin Delany wrote *Blake, or The Huts of Africa* with an aggressive protagonist.

Meanwhile, southerners offered their own versions of slavery, including William Gilmore Simms’s *Woodcraft,* which promoted the loyalty of slaves and the responsibility of slave owners as a model society. George Fitzhugh defended the slave system against the dehumanizing wage system of the North, in which workers had no protections.

The Changing South

Hinton Helper’s *Impending Crisis* asserted that the southern economy was fundamentally unsound, undermining the livelihoods of non-slaveholders, depressing the wages of white workers, and depriving the region of public services, such as schools and hospitals. The book was banned across the South, and did nothing to change the region’s views on slavery.

During the 1850s, about one-quarter of white southerners owned slaves, but this minority wielded disproportionate social and political influence. Cotton accounted for over half the dollar value of all U.S. exports, and because northern textile mills relied on southern cotton, some northern congressmen held southern sympathies. As corn and wheat replaced tobacco in the Upper South, the need for slave labor diminished, and slaves continued to be sold south to cotton-dominated regions. Yet even as the slave population overall grew, so did the free black population. And though cotton prospered, the South lacked diversified commerce. Planters complained that they were land rich but cash poor, but much of their land was, in fact, mortgaged to banks in the North and England.

The large black-to-white ratio in many parts of the South meant that African Americans exerted surprising influence. The interdependence between slaves and owners was so intricate that one historian calls it “a world they made together.” The workings of the Cocke plantation, managed by slave Lucy Skipwith, exemplified unequal power and interdependence, but the lives of most slaves and masters reveal a precarious balance between control and violence. For the 200,000 free black people in the South, living largely in cities, life was also precarious. A few, however, acquired substantial property—including slaves.

Black Exiles Abroad and at Home

The number of hospitable destinations for free black people shrank in the 1850s. Midwestern states imposed taxes on them and forbade them from entry. Other states revoked the black franchise until only in New England and Wisconsin could black men vote. Black leaders thus debated their options—emigration to Canada, escape to the American frontier, or departure for the shores of Haiti, Central America, and Africa.

A large black exile community developed in Ontario, promoted by Delany and James Holly, whose American Emigration Society endorsed Canada. Here, some 5,000 black emigrants found sanctuary—and discrimination. Yet they established schools and newspapers and debated issues in black education. When Mary Ann Shadd assumed editorship of the *Provincial Freeman,* she was the first female newspaper editor, black or white, in the United States. Black emigrants to the American West also experienced discrimination, even though the abolitionist spirit in California was strong.

Sectional Crisis

While some black Americans chose emigration, others, like Frederick Douglass turned to political methods to end slavery and gain citizenship, arguing that the U.S. Constitution should be enforced. But Douglass's increasing commitment to separate black organizations drew him away from black leaders who believed in biracial cooperation.

White people were also increasingly split over the slavery question. Stephen A. Douglas's solution of popular sovereignty, enacted for Kansas and Nebraska, produced border wars between settlers. The New England Emigrant Aid Society sent radical white abolitionists to these territories, including John Brown and his sons. Party alignments shifted as remnants of the Liberty and Free Soil parties formed the new antislavery Republican Party. On the Senate floor, Preston Brooks beat Charles Sumner senseless.

Then the Supreme Court's *Dred Scott* decision increased northern fears of slave power. Upholding the property rights of slaveholders, it overturned the Missouri Compromise, banned slaves from using the courts, and proclaimed that neither slaves nor their descendants could ever be citizens. Public debates between Douglas and Abraham Lincoln, running for the Senate from Illinois, focused attention on the *Dred Scott* decision, on popular sovereignty, and on the impending crisis.

Shortly thereafter, John Brown took action, staging a raid at Harper's Ferry, Virginia, that he hoped would arm slaves and instigate a slave uprising. Brown had spoken to the Canadian refugees; he had consulted with Tubman and Douglass and had the financial support of some abolitionists. But when the insurrection began not one local African American joined in. Brown was tried for treason and hanged. Yet abolitionists heralded Brown as noble, his raid as righteous, so that he accomplished more in death than he had in life. As white Americans came to perceive slaves' lives as intertwined with their own, the national crisis was at hand.

LEARNING OBJECTIVES

Students should be able to

- examine the heightening of racial tensions during the 1850s.
- identify the arguments about the power of the federal government and state governments.
- discuss how arguments for and against slavery became more entrenched.
- describe the legal status of free blacks.
- recognize the impact of abolitionist literature and slave narratives on the debate over slavery.

IDENTIFICATIONS

Explain the significance of each:

1. Christiana Riot
2. Fugitive Slave Act of 1850
3. Hinton Rowan Helper
4. Underground Railroad
5. Harriet Tubman
6. Levi Coffin
7. Anthony Burns
8. William and Ellen Craft
9. Solomon Northup
10. Sojourner Truth
11. William C. Nell
12. William Wells Brown
13. Margaret Garner
14. Harriet Beecher Stowe
15. *Uncle Tom's Cabin*
16. *The Impending Crisis in the South and How to Meet It*
17. Hopewell Plantation

18. Free African American slave-owners
19. American Colonization Society
20. Mary Ann Shadd
21. Free Black communities in Canada
22. Biddy Mason
23. "Moral Suasion"
24. Kansas-Nebraska Act
25. John Brown
26. "Bleeding Kansas"
27. Dred Scott Decision
28. Lincoln-Douglass Debates
29. Harper's Ferry

MULTIPLE CHOICE QUESTIONS

1. What is true about Christiana, Pennsylvania and the events in 1851?
   A. The town had 3,000 African Americans, some free and some were fugitive slaves who provided refuge to run-away slaves.
   B. On September 11, 1851 slave owner Edward Gorsuch, accompanied by federal marshals, came to Christiana to capture Joshua Kite and several other slaves who had run away two years earlier.
   C. Gorsuch was killed and his son was badly wounded. White antislavery Quakers provided assistance to Kite and several others as they fled to Canada.
   D. The Christiana Riot, as it came to be known, struck terror in the hearts of slaveholders while inspiring hope and pride in African Americans. For once, it was black men – not white – who had prevailed.
   E. All of the above statements are true.

2. The Fugitive Slave Act that accompanied the Compromise of 1850 stated that slave owners had the right to go into free states and free territory to capture their run-away slaves. It further stated that it was the duty of law enforcement agents, as well as private citizens, to detain the slave until the slave-owner could come to claim his property and return him to bondage. The act had all of the following effects EXCEPT:
   A. The new policy raised tensions for many Americans, North and South, black and white.
   B. The fears for Northerners and Southerners included: federal authority versus states' powers; constitutional protections of private property;
   C. Black fugitives had anxiety over getting enough distance from slave states to avoid apprehension; and individual citizens protested against encroaching federal power.
   D. Slave owners did not have any more problems capturing their run-away slaves after the Fugitive Slave Act was passed.

3. All of the following statements about the Underground Railroad are true EXCEPT:
   A. The Underground Railroad was a locomotive that carried slaves to freedom in the North.
   B. It was a network of stations (houses, barns, buildings) where run-away slaves could sleep by day and travel by night to the next "station."
   C. Harriet Tubman, a fugitive slave, made approximately 36 trips back into the South to personally lead over 300 slaves to freedom via the Underground Railroad.
   D. Of the estimated 100,00 former slaves who passed through the Underground Railroad between 1820 and 1860, probably three-fourths of them escaped after the 1850 Fugitive Slave Act intensified slaves' desperation and Underground Railroad conductors' commitment.

4. In what areas did most slaves who utilized the Underground Railroad originate?
   A. South Carolina, where conditions were the worst
   B. Mississippi and Alabama
   C. New Orleans, since they had access to the Mississippi
   D. The border states

5. How did William and Ellen Craft escape from slavery?
   A. Ellen passed for a sickly white man, accompanied by his slave, William.
   B. They killed their master and several people along the way.
   C. They escaped with the assistance of Harriet Tubman and the Underground Railroad.
   D. All of the above are true.

6. What eventually happened to the Crafts?
   A. Like all other slaves found under the Fugitive Slave Act, they were returned to their former owner and severely punished.
   B. They were killed as they tried to return to the South to retrieve their children.
   C. They escaped, with the help of abolitionists in Boston, to England.
   D. They fled to Cuba.

7. What was the result of fugitive slave Anthony Burns's case?
   A. Burns was arrested in Boston, tried and returned to his master.
   B. Many whites, even conservative ones, were very disturbed by the image of Burns being taken back into bondage.
   C. President Fillmore called out the federal military to ensure that Burns was returned to slavery.
   D. All of the above are true.

8. Toni Morrison's novel *Beloved* (and movie by Oprah Winfrey of the same name) was based on the true story of the fugitive slave Margaret Garner. What does her story reveal to us about fugitive slaves?
   A. The Underground Railroad worked very well.
   B. Some slaves were very brave, and would return many times to the South to help others escape.
   C. Some despised slavery so much that they were willing to kill their children rather than have them grow up slaves.
   D. Black women continued to face sexual exploitation even outside of slavery.

9. This well known abolitionist was born a slave in upstate New York and eventually ''walked" away from her master. She changed her name because of the work she did as an orator for the abolitionist cause and her cause for women's rights. She is known for her statement, "Ain't I a woman?" Whites said that she was the "only colored woman to gain a national reputation as a speaker in the years before the Civil War."
   A. Harriet Beecher Stowe
   B. Harriet Tubman
   C. Sojourner Truth
   D. Phillis Wheatley

10. Who wrote the anti-slavery novel *Uncle Tom's Cabin?*
   A. Frederick Douglass
   B. Harriet Beecher Stowe
   C. William Lloyd Garrison
   D. David Walker

11. Which of the following statements is true about the novel *Uncle Tom's Cabin?*
   A. The book forced many Northerners to understand the horrors of slavery.
   B. It inspired little reaction in the South, since no one heard about it there.
   C. The Uncle Tom character was a pawn and willing ally of whites against his fellow slaves
   D. The author actually had no knowledge of slavery, and had based the story solely on his /her imagination.

12. All of the following were African American writers during the antebellum period who used their talents to get the story out for emancipation/abolition <u>EXCEPT</u>
   A. William C. Nell.
   B. Solomon Northup.
   C. William Wells Brown.
   D. Francis Ellen Watkins.
   E. All of the above.

13. Hinton Rowan Helper, a white North Carolinian, wrote *The Impending Crisis in the South and How to Meet It* in 1857 in which he looked at slavery from an economic viewpoint. He eventually fled the South after publication of his book because planters were furious at his claims. Which of the following points were included in his book?

    A. The vast majority of southern whites (75%) did not own any slaves, and they would be better off financially if slavery did not exist.
    B. By depressing the employment opportunities and wages of white workers, slavery kept southern industries and ports from expanding.
    C. The unfair tax system was set up to support the planter at the expense of the poor white subsistence farmer.
    D. Helper argued that slavery deprived the South of funds for schools, roads, libraries, newspapers, and industries.
    E. All of the above.

14. Which of the following is true concerning black migration during the 1850s?

    A. The Canadian government, motivated by the hope that new black communities would provide a buffer zone between white Canadians and rebellious Indians, offered citizenships and the franchise to black immigrants after only three years' residency.
    B. By 1860 about 5,000 black immigrants had moved to Canada. Many of them lived in roughly nine free black towns established on the Canadian border near Lake Erie.
    C. By 1860 several thousand African Americans reached California. Another hundred made it to the Oregon Territory. In both regions slavery was outlawed. Biddy Mason and Mifflin W. Gibbs were two of the more colorful black westerners.
    D. All of the above.

15. Regarding slavery, what was the significance of the Kansas-Nebraska Act?

    A. It had nothing to do with slavery.
    B. It outlawed slavery in all remaining American territory.
    C. It repealed the Missouri Compromise line, with the possibility that slavery would be allowed in areas it never had before.
    D. None of the above statements are true.

16. What was the main issue in the Dred Scott case?

    A. Whether all slaves should be free or not
    B. Whether a slave taken into free territory was free
    C. Whether a slave woman could be legally raped by a white man
    D. Whether the abolitionist could continue to use mass mailing as a major Strategy

17. In 1846, the Missouri local courts had ruled Scott to be free, but after the Fugitive Slave Act of 1850 and the hysteria that followed, the Missouri Supreme Court overturned the decision in 1852. After five more years of litigation in the Dred Scott case, the U.S. Supreme Court handed down which of the following rulings?
    A. The judges said Scott was not free, because to free him would deprive his owner of property without due process of law.
    B. The court declared that slaves were not entitled to use the courts, as only citizens had that right.
    C. The justices maintained that neither slaves nor their descendants could ever be citizens.
    D. All of the above.

18. In 1858 in the state of Illinois, Abraham Lincoln, a relatively unknown Republican candidate, debated Stephen Douglas, the well known Democratic incumbent candidate, for the U.S. Senate seat from Illinois. What were the main issues in the Lincoln-Douglas debates?
    A. The discovery of gold in California
    B. Slavery and race
    C. Secession of the south
    D. The expansion of the powers of the federal government

19. Which of the following is <u>NOT</u> true about Lincoln and Douglas on the issue of slavery?
    A. Douglas was a proponent of popular sovereignty (voters in the area should decide on the slave issue for that area), and thought masters should be able to bring their slaves anywhere.
    B. Lincoln felt that slavery was morally wrong, but he did not advocate abolition in states where it already existed. He proposed that slavery not be allowed in new territories being added to the Union.
    C. Lincoln and Douglass both pushed for immediate emancipation of all slaves in the Union.
    D. Douglas won the Senate seat, but Lincoln won nationwide attention as a result of these debates.

20. What was John Brown's purpose in his raid of Harper's Ferry in 1859?
    A. Secure weapons at the U.S. arsenal and arm slaves from nearby Virginia plantations to join with his army in a rebellion
    B. Establish a separate, independent black nation within the United States
    C. A is true but not B
    D. Both A and B are true

21. Who supported John Brown's efforts financially?
    A. Most white Northerners donated some money.
    B. A few wealthy abolitionists and black leaders
    C. A few Southerners who were sick of the troubles over slavery
    D. All of the above

22. What was <u>NOT</u> a result of John Brown's raid?
    A. Many of the participants in the raid were killed.
    B. The raid pushed the country toward civil war by intensifying feelings on both sides.
    C. John Brown escaped to later fight for the North in the Civil War.
    D. All of the above are true.

THOUGHT QUESTIONS

1. Why did many abolitionists hold John Brown up as a hero, while Southerners viewed him as a terrorist?

2. Why were Southerners who did not own slaves willing to fight, if necessary, to maintain the "peculiar institution?"

ANSWER KEY MULTIPLE CHOICE QUESTIONS

1. E
2. D
3. A
4. D
5. A
6. C
7. D
8. C
9. C
10 B
11. A
12. E
13. E
14. D
15. C
16. B
17. D
18. B
19. C
20. D
21. B
22. C

CHAPTER 10 *Civil War and the Promises of Freedom: The Turbulent 1860s*

CHAPTER SUMMARY

Opening Vignette: Martin Delany Becomes First U.S. Army Major

Once despairing of seeing an end to slavery in the United States, Martin Delany had settled in Canada and then planned to resettle black Americans in Africa. But like thousands of others, his life was redirected by the Civil War. Pressing to serve in the Union's fighting force, in February 1865 he was commissioned the U.S. Army's first black major.

"A White Man's War"

In 1860, Republican Abraham Lincoln was elected president. While southerners viewed him as an abolitionist, black Americans knew he only opposed the extension of slavery into western territories and did not intend to interfere with it where it existed. Black leaders, including Frederick Douglass, were skeptical. But the cotton states in the Deep South, feeling excluded from a system that could choose a president without their support, seceded from the union, formed a confederacy, and began seizing federal forts and arsenals. When Lincoln sent food supplies to Fort Sumter in Charleston harbor, southern militia fired on the fort, and it surrendered. Lincoln called for troops, and states in the Upper South seceded. Four slave states did not secede, accepting Lincoln's claim that he was more interested in maintaining federal authority than in ending slavery.

Now Douglass was optimistic that the war would end slavery, but the thousands of free black Americans who volunteered for military service were turned away, told that they were not wanted in this "white man's war."

War and Freedom

Soon after the war started, fugitive slaves began arriving at Union forts, where generals such as Benjamin Butler and John C. Frémont declared them contraband—enemy property seized in wartime—and put them to work as cooks and laborers, and sometimes as armed soldiers.

War brought new roles to southern slaves. Some seized freedom, others still labored for the Confederacy, while some, such as Benjamin Montgomery, managed abandoned plantations. Pilot Robert Smalls delivered a Charleston steamship to the Union navy. In the Sea Islands, thousands of slaves whose masters had fled still worked in the fields, but for the Union army. While northern abolitionists, such as Charlotte Forten, came to provide food, clothing, and education, many former slaves felt that freedom did not bring much change to their everyday lives. In a Mississippi contraband camp, one-third died from malnutrition and disease.

Emancipation as Military and Political Strategy

As war continued, Union leaders concluded that African Americans could have immense strategic value in dealing with the challenges of federal control and confidence in federal authority. Trying to strike a balance between abolitionist pressure and retaining the loyal slave states, Lincoln proposed compensated emancipation, but Congress turned him down. Congress abolished slavery in the District of Columbia and established diplomatic relations with Haiti and Liberia. There were other tokens—Henry Highland Garnet was issued a passport as a *citizen*, and William C. Nell was appointed a postal clerk. But Lincoln's clumsy overtures toward African Americas were undermined by his plan to relocate slaves to Central America. Black leaders remained skeptical and frustrated.

The Union victory at Antietam in September 1862 finally prompted Lincoln to stop waffling on the fate of slaves. His preliminary Emancipation Proclamation was designed to only free slaves in areas where the Union had no control and only if the war did not end by the end of the year. Despite its limitations, emancipation's promise lifted black spirits.

"Men of Color, To Arms!"

Delany responded to the Emancipation Proclamation by proposing a private black army to aid the Union, but before he could organize it, Lincoln, recognizing that the "white man's war" lacked enough white recruits, authorized the first black regiment—the Massachusetts Fifty-fourth. Now black leaders recruited black men to the war effort; eventually 180,000 black enlisted men and 7,000 officers served the Union army, about 10 percent of the North's fighting force. Black soldiers fought bravely at Fort Wagner and won Congressional Medals of Honor, but many had labor assignments not unlike the drudgery of slavery. Not until June 1864 were they paid the same as white soldiers. At Fort Pillow, 300 who were captured by Confederate troops were killed as "insurrectionists," for Confederate policy did not recognize them as soldiers. For black women and children who fled to the Union lines, freedom brought heavy labor assignments. While some got help from northern relief agencies, most had to fend for themselves.

1863: The Tide Turns

The Union victory at Gettysburg foreshadowed northern victory, ending the possibility of English and French support for the Confederacy and, with Lincoln's Gettysburg Address, hallowing the idea that the war effort was "dedicated to the proposition that all men are created equal." Yet anti-draft riots, most notably in New York, exposed the inequality of a draft system in which those who could afford it could hire a substitute. Racial anxieties and fear of job competition prompted white workers to attack black neighborhoods.

In 1864, General William T. Sherman's victories in Georgia secured the presidential election for Lincoln, but barely. His Special Field Order No. 15 granted confiscated land in Florida, Georgia, and South Carolina to black families, raising hopes that the federal government would provide all freed people with "forty acres and a mule."

An Incomplete Victory

Black people rejoiced at the southern surrender in April 1865, but within days, Lincoln was killed by Confederate sympathizer John Wilkes Booth. Delany and other black Americans memorialized Lincoln as their savior, helping create a legend that remained untarnished for more than a century. In December, the Thirteenth Amendment ended slavery everywhere in the United States, but it did not include the franchise.

Thousands of freed black Americans sought lost family members, separated by slave sales, escape, and exile. Benjamin Montgomery and his family, sent by Union commanders to Ohio, returned home. Federal troops occupied the South to impose civil order, and the Freedmen's Bureau tried to restore the economy by allocating work, supplies, and abandoned and confiscated southern lands among freed black people. It also helped families reunite and challenged Maryland's oppressive apprentice system for black children. Its victory in the Supreme Court re-established African Americans' ability to seek justice in the courts.

Maryland's system of separate laws for black people was part of a larger southern legal pattern establishing Black Codes that restricted black people's movement, economic and social prospects, and access to legal redress. Even the contracts promoted by the Freedmen's Bureau bound black workers to repetitive tasks, long hours, and low wages. The sharecropping system, in which the landowner provided land and possibly seeds, supplies, and work animals in return for a share of the crop, was blatant exploitation, keeping black people perpetually in debt to the owner and therefore tied to the land. For sharecroppers, the new conditions of freedom did not seem free.

Though overwhelmed by land and labor issues, the Freedmen's Bureau did a better job of distributing food, medical care, and especially education, establishing over 4,000 schools. At Hampton, the curriculum focused on self-discipline, hygiene, and manual skills; at Howard, students got a liberal education and even degrees in law and medicine.

Even while black southerners pursued self-improvement, white southerners formed hate organizations such as the Ku Klux Klan, which used night raids and threats to keep blacks from economic advancement or political participation. Race-hatred showed black southerners what black northerners had long understood: true equality came only with political power. Even during the war black northerners had begun organizing Equal Rights Leagues that insisted the war was about citizenship as well as slavery. The Fourteenth Amendment, ratified in 1868, still did not secure the franchise. For decades, black people equated manhood with the right to go to the polls.

LEARNING OBJECTIVES

Students should be able to

- describe the impact of the Civil War on slaves as well as all Americans.
- discuss the role played by African Americans during the war.
- explain the importance of the constitutional amendments that came out of the Civil War.
- discuss the backlash against the end of slavery.

IDENTIFICATIONS

Explain the significance of each:

1. Martin Delaney
2. Frederick Douglass
3. Fort Sumter
4. "Contraband"
5. Benjamin Butler
6. "A White Man's War"
7. CSA
8. Preliminary Emancipation Proclamation
9. Jefferson Davis
10. Border states or "loyal slave states"
11. 54th Massachusetts Regiment
12. First South Carolina Volunteers
13. John C. Freemont
14. Field Order #15
15. Congressional Confiscation Act
16. Wade-Davis Bill
17. *Ex Parte Vallandighan*
18. Freedmen's Bureau
19. Port Royal Experiment
20. Gettysburg
21. James Henry Gooden
22. General Ulysses Grant
23. General William Tecumseh Sherman

24. General Robert E. Lee

25. Fort Pillow

26. Thirteenth Amendment

27. John Wilkes Booth

28. Ku Klux Klan

29. Fourteenth Amendment

30. Black Codes

MULTIPLE CHOICE QUESTIONS

1. Which of the following statements is true about Martin Delaney?
   A. He was a free black abolitionist of means who had become disgruntled over the possibilities of ending slavery in the United States and as a result moved to Canada. He then planned to resettle black Americans in Africa.
   B. Delaney went to Africa in 1859 and founded the Niger Valley Exploring Party. He also went to England to drum up support for his plan to bring African Americans to Niger.
   C. Delaney returned to the U.S. in 1860 only to find that the country was on the verge of civil war. His plans were redirected as he pushed to serve in the Union army once war broke out.
   D. In February 1865, near the end of the war, Delaney was commissioned the U.S. Army's first black major.
   E. All of the above.

2. How did Frederick Douglass, as well as many other knowledgeable African Americans, feel about Abraham Lincoln and his views on slavery?
   A. Many African Americans knew that while Lincoln openly said that slavery was morally wrong, he did not advocate abolition.
   B. Frederick Douglass felt that Lincoln wanted to keep slavery from new states and territories, but did not propose to interfere with slavery where it already existed.
   C. Black leaders were skeptical about the plight of slavery when Lincoln was elected President in 1860.
   D. Black leaders loved Lincoln for the most part and rejoiced when he was elected President in 1860.
   E. All except D are correct.

3. What is <u>NOT</u> true about "contraband?"
   A. The term refers to "enemy property."
   B. Run-away slaves were considered contraband by Union troops.
   C. Union troops did not want to have anything to do with "contraband."
   D. Union troops gave refuge to run-away slaves knowing that this would eventually hurt the planter and the Southern cause.

4. Which of the following statements is <u>NOT</u> true?
   A. South Carolina was the first slaveholding state to secede from the Union in December, 1860, immediately after the Electoral College certified Lincoln's election.
   B. All of the slaveholding states had seceded from the Union by April, 1861.
   C. By February, 1861, seven Southern states had seceded from the Union and formed their own country, the Confederates States of America.
   D. In April, 1861, after the firing on Fort Sumter, four other slaveholding states joined the CSA bringing it to a total of 11 states.

5. What Union General began the policy of accepting runaway slaves as "contraband?"
   A. General Benjamin Butler
   B. General Ulysses Grant
   C. General William Tecumseh Sherman
   D. General Winfield Scott

6. Who did Confederates choose as their President?
   A. Nathan Bedford Forrest
   B. Robert E. Lee
   C. Jefferson Davis
   D. John Wilkes Booth

7. What was Lincoln's aim of the Civil War when it began in 1861?
   A. To free the slaves
   B. To preserve the Union, without regard to ending slavery
   C. To preserve the Union and to free the slaves
   D. Lincoln was completely surprised by the south's secession, and had no initial aims.

8. How were black volunteers greeted by the United States government in 1861?
   A. The government, realizing it would need all available manpower, accepted them reluctantly.
   B. The government accepted the early volunteers, but only with great reluctance.
   C. The government immediately sent them into the South to serve as spies.
   D. The government refused to enlist them.

9. What did Abraham Lincoln initially think was the appropriate long term solution to slavery?

   A. Lincoln thought that slaves should be freed immediately, without compensation.
   B. Lincoln thought no slaves should be freed, since that would damage property rights.
   C. Lincoln wanted to compensate masters for their slaves and then send the slaves out of the United States.
   D. None of the above are true.

10. Which of the following is NOT true about border states or "loyal slave states?"

    A. These are the slaveholding states that did not secede from the Union.
    B. They are the states of Missouri, Maryland, Delaware, Kentucky, and later West Virginia.
    C. These are the states that surround the Confederacy and wanted to be part of the CSA.
    D. These are slaveholding states that the Confederacy hoped would join its cause while the Union wanted to make sure that nothing was done to cause them to leave the U.S.

11. Which of the following regiments were NOT made up of black soldiers during the Civil War?

    A. First South Carolina Volunteers
    B. 9th U.S. Cavalry Unit
    C. 54th Massachusetts Regiment
    D. Second South Carolina Volunteers

12. Which of the following statements are true about black military service during the Civil War?

    A. Occasionally, black men served in integrated units in the army.
    B. White officers were often ready to command black troops, since they received more pay.
    C. Black soldiers were paid less, since whites thought they would only be used for menial work.
    D. None of the above are true.

13. What sacrifice did the men of the 54th Massachusetts make to protest race discrimination?

    A. They went on a hunger strike to protest unequal treatment.
    B. They had the first sit-in, at the White House, and were arrested and charged with treason.
    C. They said they would accept no pay unless it was equal to white men.
    D. The 54th Massachusetts men made no protest against race discrimination, as they were an all-white regiment.

14. What was Special Field Order #15?

A. It was an order written by General William T. Sherman promising "40 acres and a mule" to the head of newly freed black families.
B. The land involved was confiscated land in South Carolina, Georgia and Florida abandoned by white families fleeing the Union armies.
C. Much of the land was parceled out only to be reclaimed by the descendants of white families as ordered by law.
D. All of the above.

15. What was the Port Royal Experiment?

A. Port Royal, the largest of the Sea Islands in South Carolina, was turned into an all-black town in 1862 after whites fled the oncoming Union army.
B. Former slaves were paid very meager wages for their labor on the plantation. Federal officials and Northern abolitionists operated the town as an experiment researching the ability of former slaves to take care of themselves.
C. Education was stressed. Many ex slaves in Port Royal complained that the rewards were few for the hard labor performed, and some of them were not compensated as much as they had been under their former masters.
D. The managers reaped a tidy profit from the town and the Experiment was considered a success. However blacks, as a whole, in Port Royal did not feel that so-called freedom had changed their lives much.
E. All of the above.

16. All of the following happened at Fort Pillow EXCEPT:

A. Union troops were defeated there in April, 1864, by Confederate forces under the command of General Nathan Bedford Forrest.
B. Forrest ordered his men to kill all 300 black troops after they had surrendered and were unarmed.
C. This was one of the most horrendous examples of the Confederates' blanket policy of treating captured black troops as "insurrectionists" rather than as POWs.
D. All of the above statements are true.

17. Which of the statements below is true?

A. At Appomattox Court House in Virginia in April, 1865, General Ulysses S. Grant surrendered to General Robert E. Lee, thus bringing an end to the Civil War.
B. At Appomattox Court House, President Abraham Lincoln received the surrender from President Jefferson Davis.
C. At Appomattox Court House in Virginia in April, 1865, General Robert E. Lee surrendered to General Ulysses S. Grant, thus bringing an end to the Civil War.
D. At Appomattox Court House, Confederate General Stonewall Jackson was mistakenly killed by a Confederate sharpshooter.

18. The Thirteenth Amendment to the constitution provided for
    A. the abolition of slavery throughout the United States.
    B. the abolition of slavery in states still in rebellion against the Union.
    C. the right of African Americans to vote.
    D. citizenship rights for all African Americans.

19. This man assassinated President Lincoln five days after the war ended as the President was attending a performance at Ford's Theater in D.C.
    A. Lee Harvey Oswald
    B. John Wilkes Booth
    C. Benedict Arnold
    D. Aaron Burr

20. As a result of the establishment of Black Codes by local white officials and the harassment by the Ku Klux Klan to newly freed blacks as well as other issues, Congress passed the Fourteenth Amendment to the constitution which provided for
    A. the right of citizenship to all persons in the U. S. regardless to race, sex, or previous condition of servitude, not to be denied.
    B. the abolition of slavery throughout the United States.
    C. the right to vote, not be denied to any person on the basis of race, sex or previous condition of servitude.
    D. All of the above.

THOUGHT QUESTIONS

1. How did the Emancipation Proclamation change the course of the Civil War? Was the Proclamation a military strategy? Was it a foreign policy strategy? Was it based on moral principles?

2. Many people think that Abraham Lincoln freed the slaves, and have given him the reputation of the Great Emancipator. What was the real meaning and effect of the Emancipation Proclamation and Lincoln's view of blacks?

3. How did slaves react when they learned of their freedom?

ANSWER KEY MULTIPLE CHOICE QUESTIONS

1. E
2. E
3. C
4. B
5. A
6. C
7. B
8. D
9. C
10. C
11. B
12. C
13. C
14. D
15. E
16. D
17. C
18. A
19. B
20. A

CHAPTER 11 *Post-Civil War Reconstruction: A New National Era*

CHAPTER SUMMARY

Opening Vignette: Emanuel Fortune Testifies Before Congress

In 1871, Florida Republican Emanuel Fortune told a congressional committee that despite constitutional guarantees, threats and violence prevented black southerners from political participation. Without political rights, black southerners could not achieve their goals of economic self-sufficiency for themselves and education for their children.

Postwar Reconstruction

Radical Republicans, dominating Congress after the war, aimed to protect and promote the interests of black southerners and to punish white southerners. Reconstruction Acts sent federal troops into the South to maintain order, required former Confederate states to guarantee black male suffrage, and made ratification of the Fourteenth Amendment, which affirmed black people's citizenship, a condition of representation in Congress. Abraham Lincoln had proposed a milder form of Reconstruction, and under his successor Andrew Johnson black rights became the focal point of a contest between the Congress and the executive. In an impeachment trial, the Radical Republicans failed to remove Johnson, but the contest for power between the branches of government—ostensibly about black issues—only diverted federal attention from black people's needs.

In a bitter irony, southern black men, so recently liberated from slavery, had more opportunities for political leadership than did black northerners. As voters in northern states denied black men the franchise, former abolitionists and black leaders joined in Equal Rights Leagues to fight for full political equality. The 1868 elections brought more moderate Republicans to power, and they proposed the Fifteenth Amendment, prohibiting states from limiting the franchise due to "race, color, or previous condition of servitude." Former Confederate states now had to ratify this new amendment, and Mississippi, one of the first to do so, sent Hiram Revels to the Senate, the first black American in Congress.

The Fourteenth and Fifteenth amendments split the old alliance between black rights and women's rights. The "black men first" strategy specified that males only were citizens, outraging Elizabeth Cady Stanton. Opposing the amendments, Stanton found herself linked to anti-black forces. The issue split the women's rights movement into rival organizations that further split along racial lines, and Mary Ann Shadd Cary and others formed the Colored Woman's Progressive Franchise Association.

Elected Black Leaders

In Congress, Revels's seat was challenged, and he and the six other African Americans found their new power limited. Yet most were pragmatic, using compromise and negotiation to promote education, full citizenship, and patronage for black people. Those who refused to compromise learned that their vote wielded little influence without white allies. On the local level, too, black leaders used compromise and negotiation to gain white support and advance their agenda. Martin Delany, for example, advocated black-white alliances and supported planter Wade Hampton for governor of South Carolina.

In the postwar era, southern politics took one of three forms—the political middle, which, like Hampton, hoped to modernize the South with a diversified economy and new industry; the political right, which sought to hold former slaves in place as laborers on the land; and the radical left, which promoted an alliance of poor people across racial lines and sometimes embraced socialism. Most black leaders, like Delany, cultivated political connections with white moderates; only a few, such as Lucy Parsons, joined the socialist ranks; and all avoided the political right as best they could.

In northern cities, discrimination, especially in transportation, and even violence were evidence that northern white Americans wanted black people to stay "in their place." But white backlash was much more violent in the South, where the Ku Klux Klan murdered an estimated 20,000 African Americans between 1868 and 1876. Enforcement Acts, aiming to protect black voters against Klan violence, were ineffective, though they did bring black spokesmen like Fortune to Congress to testify.

The Freedmen's Bank

The Freedmen's Bank, chartered by Congress, was intended to help black people save money and secure loans, but when unwise speculation caused it to fail and Congress would not save it, the savings of thousands of African Americans evaporated. For many, the failure was evidence that the federal government would not support black initatives, foreshadowing the disinclination of the federal government to protect black rights.

Washington, DC, in the New National Era

Though symbolizing both hope and disappointment, the national capital became a magnet for African Americans seeking employment and federal production. After the war, black people constituted 30 percent of Washington's population. A black elite—about 2 percent of this 30 percent—included professionals, often of mixed race background, from families that had been free for a generation or more. Frederick Douglass, Frances Ellen Watkins Harper, Maria Stewart, and Charlotte Forten were among city's essayists, writers, and public speakers. Shopkeepers and service workers formed the core of the middle class, but more than three-quarters of the city's African Americans were poor, living in alleys in conditions as bleak as endured under slavery. Sojourner Truth and Mary Ann Shadd Cary, Howard University's first female law student, spoke for their interests, arguing for access to education, manual training, and employment. But increasingly, black political leaders—economically well off and circulating in their own social clubs and organizations—lost touch with the needs of ordinary black people.

The District of Columbia's local government offered opportunities for employment, and loyal black Republican supporters were rewarded with political patronage positions. Steady wages allowed for middle-class lifestyles for some and elevated others to elite status. African Americans relocating here and to other cities, too, found they could make some economic progress and begin participating in local politics. Many cities had enough black residents to support a black press.

The End of Reconstruction

As Republican power began to wane in the early 1870s, African American progress began to wane as well. Democrats took over state and local governments in the South, a development hailed by white southerners as "redemption." By the Compromise of 1877, settling the contested presidential election in 1876, federal troops were withdrawn from the South altogether, and federal intervention in southern state affairs ceased. The Supreme Court also limited black advances. In the *Slaughterhouse Cases* it weakened the scope of the Fourteenth Amendment by ruling that states had the right to define citizenship, and in 1883 it overturned the Civil Rights Act of 1875, distinguishing between political rights and social rights, which it claimed no power to enforce.

African Americans on the Move

Increasingly, black people chose to leave the South rather than endure violence—including rape, murder, and mutilation. Some, called Exodusters, took advantage of the 1862 Homestead Act and headed for Kansas, founding all-black towns such as Nicodemus. Others went farther west, to the frontiers in Colorado and North Dakota and even to the Pacific Coast. But some white southerners, seeking to retain the South's cheap labor force, sought to block their plans, and from Washington, Douglass urged black families to stay in the South, where their numbers might be large enough to exert political power and influence.

Other black Americans, driven by the same hope and frustration that motivated western migration, looked to Africa. Delany revived his dream of claiming a black nationality there, and with AME minister Henry McNeal Turner, he recruited settlers for Liberia. Though their Liberian Exodus Company collapsed, the image of an African homecoming remained in the black imagination and future generations would try again.

LEARNING OBJECTIVES

Students should be able to

- differentiate between the various Reconstruction plans.
- explain the significance of the Fifteenth Amendment.
- explain the factors leading to the end of Reconstruction.
- discuss the challenges facing ex-slaves and their strategies for coping with them.

IDENTIFICATIONS

Explain the significance of each:

1. Emanuel Fortune
2. Civil Rights Act of 1866
3. Hiram Revels
4. Presidential Reconstruction 1865 - 1867
5. Andrew Johnson
6. Edwin Stanton
7. Impeachment
8. Radical or Congressional Reconstruction
9. Thaddeus Stevens
10. Charles Sumner
11. Fifteenth Amendment
12. Frances Ellen Watkins Harper
13. Blanche K. Bruce
14. Pinckney Benton Stewart Pinchback
15. Wade Hampton
16. Madison Heming
17. Enforcement Acts and/or Klan Acts of 1870 and 1871
18. The Freedmen's Bank
19. African Americans and Washington, DC
20. Howard University
21. John Mercer Langston
22. Freedmen's Hospital
23. Charlotte Forten

24. The Black Elite

25. Sojourner Truth

26. Mary Ann Shadd Cary

27. The Franchise

28. The Disputed Election of 1876

29. Exodusters

30. Nat Love

31. Martin Delaney, Henry McNeal Turner and the *Azor*

MULTIPLE CHOICE QUESTIONS

1. This African American appeared before a congressional committee assigned to investigate Ku Klux Klan threats and violence against black southerners in 1871. In spite of intimidation, this political leader participated in the 1868 constitutional convention that qualified Florida to reenter the Union, and over the next 10 years he served as city marshal, Republican national convention delegate, county commissioner, clerk of the city market, and state legislator. He was
   A. Martin Delaney.
   B. Emanuel Fortune.
   C. Blanche K. Bruce.
   D. Hiram Revels.

2. Presidential Reconstruction took place between 1865 and 1867. Under this plan for restoring the former Confederate states to the Union, President Lincoln and his successor favored a lenient policy whereby once a southern state ratified the Thirteenth Amendment and a portion of the white voters took an oath of allegiance to the Union, then that state could come back into the Union with no further punishment. All of the following facts about Presidential Reconstruction are true EXCEPT:
   A. By December, 1865, most of the former Confederate states had been restored to the Union.
   B. Many former Confederate officeholders were sitting in Congress to help govern a country that they had just spent the past four years trying to destroy when Congress convened in December, 1865.
   C. Local white political leaders passed laws called "Black Codes" that severely limited the freedom of the newly freed blacks.
   D. The Freedmen's Bureau established schools, provided assistance, and helped African Americans adjust to the new life.
   E. By 1866 African Americans could sue in court, could vote, and could hold public office in most Southern states.

3. What was the first concern of many African Americans once they achieved freedom?
    A. Retaliating against former masters
    B. Reuniting with lost family members
    C. Forming churches
    D. Moving to the Northern cities

4. Who became President after Lincoln was assassinated in April, 1865?
    A. Andrew Johnson
    B. Lyndon Baines Johnson
    C. Andrew Jackson
    D. William Tecumseh Sherman
    E. Ulysses S. Grant

5. On what grounds did the Radical Republicans in Congress bring impeachment proceedings against Lincoln's successor?
    A. The president tried to remove his secretary of war Edwin Stanton. This removal was in violation of the recently passed Tenure of Office Act.
    B. The president promised to restore confiscated land to former Confederate owners - land that had been parceled out to newly freed blacks.
    C. The president vetoed Congress' Civil Rights Act of 1866 – an act that offered limited legal rights to African Americans.
    D. He also vetoed a congressional vote to renew the charter for the Freedmen's Bureau.
    E. All of the above.

6. This president held the record, before Bill Clinton, of being the only president to be impeached but not removed from office. He was one vote shy of being removed. Who was he?
    A. Andrew Jackson
    B. Ulysses S. Grant
    C. Andrew Johnson
    D. Lyndon Baines Johnson
    E. William Tecumseh Sherman

7. In 1867 Congress passed three new Reconstruction acts that brought on what is known as Radical or Congressional Reconstruction. Which of the following provisions were part of Congressional Reconstruction?
    A. The South was divided into five military districts, sending federal troops to maintain order and protect freed people.
    B. Former Confederate states were required to hold conventions to draft constitutions that guaranteed black male suffrage.
    C. Former Confederate states could send representatives to Congress only after state legislatures had voted to ratify the proposed Fourteenth Amendment.
    D. All of the above.
    E. Only A and B are correct.

8. Charles Sumner and Thaddeus Stevens were the two leading Radical Republicans in Congress. Stevens in the House and Sumner in the Senate paved the way for the passage of the Fourteenth and Fifteenth Amendments to the Constitution. Which of the following leaders of the period are NOT correctly paired with their achievements?
   - A. Hiram Revels and Blanche K. Bruce – African American U.S. Senators from the state of Mississippi
   - B. Martin Delaney and Henry McNeal Turner – 'Back to Africa' movement
   - C. Frances Ellen Watkins Harper and Mary Ann Shadd Cary – Black female Civil rights advocates
   - D. Charlotte Forten and Sojourner Truth – African American pioneers who became Exodusters

9. The Fifteenth Amendment to the Constitution provided for which of the following?
   - A. Abolition of slavery
   - B. Male Negro suffrage
   - C. Negro citizenship
   - D. An end to segregation

10. During Congressional or radical Reconstruction, African Americans participated for the first time in local, state and national politics. In Congress eventually 22 African Americans served – two in the Senate and 20 in the House. What is the highest state office to which a black man was elected in the South during Reconstruction?
    - A. Governor
    - B. State senator
    - C. Lieutenant Governor
    - D. Blacks were not elected to any state offices.

11. Which of the following statements is NOT true about black officeholders during Reconstruction?
    - A. They were always well-qualified for their office.
    - B. Only a small minority had attended college.
    - C. Some had been free before the war; some had been slaves.
    - D. Farmers and workers were well represented.

12. Which of the following men was the offspring of a union between a slave woman, Sally, and her white master, Thomas Jefferson, who went on to become the third President of the United States?
    - A. John Mercer Langston
    - B. Madison Heming
    - C. Wade Hampton
    - D. P.B.S. Pinchback

13. The Ku Klux Klan, a notorious hate group, was founded in 1866, in Pulaski, Tennessee. According to some sources, shortly after the war's end, idle planters and their sons were initiating some of their peers into a secret organization when they discovered by accident that the hoods and robes worn during pledge night frightened and/or intimidated a group of blacks. Drawing on that fear, the organization grew and continued to harass anyone who supported Reconstruction or ethnic equality, its victims were mainly blacks. Which of the following statements concerning the actions of the KKK is NOT true?

    A. Klan activity and membership was generally popular only among the poor whites who resented both elite whites and blacks.
    B. Klan actions frequently helped to eliminate Republican leadership.
    C. Klan members conducted campaigns of violence, murder and terrorism against blacks.
    D. All of the above are true.

14. What was the main impediment to enforcing laws against the Klan?

    A. Since no terrorist groups had existed before, there were no laws to deal with them.
    B. Many times, local law enforcement or white troops sided with the Klan against the blacks.
    C. There were only a very small number of men in the Klan, and they always remained secret and hidden from prosecution.
    D. The Klan's actions were almost invisible since no one reported news of the terrorism.

15. Which of the following statements about the Enforcement Acts of 1870 and 1871 are true?

    A. They made it a federal crime to interfere with someone's right to vote.
    B. They authorized the president to send in federal troops if necessary.
    C. They authorized the president to suspend the writ of habeas corpus if necessary.
    D. All of the above are true.

16. Why did the Freedmen's Savings Bank fail?

    A. The bank's black board of directors had little direct knowledge of banking practices.
    B. The bank had no support from the black community.
    C. The stock market at that point was very weak and fluctuated wildly.
    D. The white leaders of the bank invested unsoundly, and lost everything in the Panic of 1873.

17. The seat of both hope and disappointment, Washington, DC, became a magnet for black Americans. By 1870, African Americans constituted more than 30 percent of the capital city's population of 132,000. Which of the following statements about African Americans in DC are true?

    A. Drawn by the federal government and Howard University, many accomplished African Americans settled in the capital city. Frederick Douglass moved to DC and started a newspaper, then later moved into government service. John Mercer Langston moved there to direct the law curriculum at Howard University and also later got involved in government service. There were many other affluent blacks who did likewise.
    B. Many intellectuals, such as black poets, essayists, novelists, and public speakers were drawn to DC by intellectuals who were already there. The black elite of Washington, DC – around two percent of the city's black population- consisted of lawyers, doctors, teachers, publishers and business owners.
    C. Shopkeepers and service workers formed the core of DC's black middle class. They enjoyed the chance to rub shoulders not only with DC's black politicians and intellectuals but also with renowned social activists.
    D. More than three quarters of DC's black families lived in alleys next to large houses where they served as laundresses, porters, handymen, and domestic servants. In the crowded alleys near the Capitol and along the Potomac River lived those who worked in government service.
    E. All of the above.

18. Radical Reconstruction had brought important gains to black southerners: schools, varied economic possibilities, and the franchise. In 1875, Congress passed a Civil Rights act that banned discrimination in public places throughout the country. By 1876, many white Northerners had grown tired of the plight of the newly freed blacks; consequently the Presidential election of that year showed just that. Because neither candidate received the required number of electoral votes, the election was thrown in to the House of Representatives. As a result of the Compromise of 1877, Rutherford B. Hayes, a Republican, won. Which of the following concessions did Hayes have to make in order to win?

    A. He would agree to end Reconstruction by pulling military troops out of the southern states.
    B. White southerners would be able to control local elections and would be able to make local ordinances controlling such issues as black employment contracts and racial separation.
    C. Federal intervention in southern state affairs would cease and Hayes would appoint at least one southerner to the president's cabinet.
    D. A and B are correct but C is not.
    E. A, B, and C are correct.

19. Who were the Exodusters?

A. 40,000 African Americans who left the south and migrated to Kansas between the years 1870 and 1880
B. Black people, likening themselves to the biblical Hebrews that fled from bondage in Egypt, who went west with groups financed by the Kansas Exodus Joint Stock Company
C. African Americans who took advantage of the Homestead Act and moved, despite opposition from southern whites, to Nicodemus, Kansas, establishing the all-black town there
D. All of the above
E. B and C are correct

20. All of the following African Americans moved to the western frontier, found adventure and/or fortune in places such as Nebraska, Colorado, North Dakota or along the Pacific coast. Who among the following did NOT settle in the West?

A. Isom Dart
B. Nat Love
C. Nancy Lewis
D. Biddy Mason
E. All of the above-mentioned colorful characters lived on the Western Frontier.

THOUGHT QUESTIONS

1. Based on the economic, political, and social changes brought on by Reconstruction, was Reconstruction a success or a failure for African Americans?

2. How did African Americans attempt to work within the political system during Reconstruction to effect change? How were they limited?

3. How was the Freedmen's Bureau both a positive and a negative influence for the newly freed blacks? Why did Bureau members seem to want blacks to stay in agricultural positions?

ANSWER KEY MULTIPLE CHOICE QUESTIONS

1. B
2. E
3. B
4. A
5. E
6. C
7. D
8. D
9. B
10. C
11. A
12. B
13. A
14. B
15. D
16. D
17. E
18. E
19. D
20. E